Public School Confessions
True Stories
from The Front Lines of Public Education^
by Mark Wilkins

Table of Contents

Mr. Happyhands New Lesson

I Don't Have Time

The Bushwhacker

The Good Guy

Corporal Punishment

The French Substitute

High School

The Big Drug Bust

A Tale of Two Brothers

I'm Taking Roll

The Power of the Pen

*by The Prophet of Life

^contains content from Classroom Confessions 1 & 2

Preface

I am actually a teacher in the front lines of Public Education in an Urban School District in America. In my 30+ year career as a teacher, I have known a good many teachers, administrators, classified staff and students. I count many of them among my friends my friends. I have always admired the tenacity of teachers who try to shape the future of the most vulnerable in our society, often, with little support from the schools or districts they work for.

The stories that fill this book are taken from true stories that I have witnessed or have been told by colleagues during my career. I have changed names and embellished in some areas for effect but every one of these stories are derived from true events. Although I can relate numerous stories, I have chosen stories with memorable characters and what I consider interesting plots. Some are humorous, others are serious but they all play a part in the story of public education today. I have even interspersed appropriate poetic lyrics I wrote for an Alternative Rock Band made up entirely of inner city public school teachers to further deepen the experience of reading this book. I hope you enjoy reading this as much as I enjoyed writing it as a tribute to those who are on the front lines of public education.

Mark Wilkins

M.A. in Educational Leadership

The Lesson

A high school teacher decided to teach his student the work ethic. He arranged to have the student help him dig a couple of small trenches in a local park. On the appointed day, they went to the park. The teacher took a shovel he was carrying and briefly showed the student how to dig a small trench. Then he asked the student to dig one. The student complied. When the student finished digging the trench, the teacher asked him to dig another and still another after that. After the student had finished digging several small trenches he stopped. He asked the teacher a question.

"Why am I doing all of the work and you are just watching?" He asked the teacher.

"That is because I am supervising you." replied the teacher.

After another hour had passed and the student had dug several more small trenches, the teacher told him to stop.

"What did you learn from today?' He asked the student.

"I learned the meaning of a new word." replied the student.

"Is the word work?" The teacher asked in eager anticipation.

"No, "said the student the word is supervisor.

"Supervisor?" asked the teacher with a puzzled look on his face.

"Yes," said the student.

"Supervisor, I do all the work, you just watch and you get paid more than me, supervisor." The student concluded.

Her Brief Retirement

Scott had known Bertha for about 20 years. They worked together at the same high school. He taught History; she taught Spanish. When she retired the previous June she had been a bit forgetful. She told him she was worried about her future because she had no family to look after her and had just bought a new condo but didn't know anyone in the complex. Her only friend was her Chihuahua Pepi.

Scott thought about agreeing to look after her, maybe call her once a week and stop by her condo on occasion but it seemed to be a lot of extra time to invest on someone he didn't know well. Besides, he thought, she would be okay because…because…she had to and besides, these things always have a way of working themselves out.

As the next school year began, Scott thought about Bertha. He wondered how she was doing. After a few weeks rolled by he thought about asking the School's Office Manager for Bertha's phone number, so he could give her a call but whenever he had an opportunity to ask, something always came up. A couple of months went by and Scott asked the Office Manager if anyone had heard from Bertha. To his surprise, she replied that no one had heard from her. Scott asked the Office Manager for Bertha's phone number.

Another couple of months rolled by before Scott actually dialed the number. He got a message saying that the phone had been disconnected. The next day, Scott asked the Office Manager for Bertha's address. She jotted it down and handed him the paper. When Scott looked at the paper, he realized that Bertha's condo was on his way home. He had passed by it every day as he went to and from work. He decided to stop by that day on his way from work.

When Scott got off of work, he drove to the address. He parked his car and was able to get into the complex. He found his way to the building she lived in and walked up a flight of stairs to her condo on the second floor. He saw a yellow tape across the door. The Tape had the words "Police Line Do Not Cross" printed on it. He went to a neighboring apartment and knocked on the door. A woman answered and he asked her about the yellow police line tape. The lady said that about three weeks before, she smelled a bad odor and called the management. When she woke up the next morning the yellow tape was on the door.

Scott walked over to the Manager's condo but no one was home. He went home and looked through the internet typing in Bertha's first and last name. He found articles about a teacher of the year award she had won, about her retirement the previous June and then, he saw an article that disturbed him. The Headline was **Spanish Teacher Found Dead in Her Apartment with The Skeleton of a Small Dog Lying next To Her.** The article said that Bertha was found on March 27th and that the coroner estimated that she had died the previous October.

Just A Teacher

As recorded by the Alternative Rock Band
Teacherz
Lyrics by The Prophet of Life

VERSE 1

I build the future of this nation
One child at a time
I help them shape their dreams
And give them wings to fly
I educate your kids
And teach them not to hate
Teach them how to read and write
And all that you can say is

CHORUS

I'm a Teacher
But I'm your teacher
I'm just a teacher

VERSE 2

You make me jump through hoops
Get credentials and degrees
Then pay me less than those who are
Less educated than me

The conditions that I work in
Are usually third world
But you complain when I advocate
On behalf of boys and girls
CHORUS
I'm a Teacher
But I'm your teacher
I'm just a teacher

VERSE 3
Tie me down with unfunded mandates
Like No Child Left Behind
Give me a pinto budget
Expect a Cadillac ride

But its you who made the system
And you who refuse to change
And I who wonders who really
Has their priorities straight

CHORUS
I'm a Teacher
But I'm your teacher
I'm just a teacher

A Naughty Little Boy

Jake Gold was a small, shy, nerdy third grader. He often had the right answer when he raised his hand. He often asked questions that showed he was thinking ahead of the other children. He was however, the victim of a bully.

Regina Crumbie was the meanest girl in the third grade. Many of the children at 1st Street Elementary thought she was the meanest girl in the whole world. She dominated any conversation she horned her way into. She was physically aggressive with others when she didn't get her way. The only time anyone ever saw her smile was whenever one of the other children got hurt on the playground.

Regina loved Jake. She didn't love him in a classical way but she loved to flick her index finger in the back of his big ears. She flicked his ears at every opportunity. Fortunately, Regina was in the other third grade class. Jake just learned to avoid her but she would go up to him every chance she got and flick the back of his ear with her index finger.

One day, Regina showed up in Jake's class with her mother who was looked like a very proper lady. Their teacher, Mrs. Bigalow, told the class to welcome their new student Regina Crumbie. She also told them to be on their best behavior because Mrs. Crumbie came to observe the new class her daughter was in. Mrs. Bigalow sat Regina next to Jake. As Regina sat down and pulled her notebook out of her backpack, she got close to Jake and whispered in his ear.

"Now I have you all to myself for the rest of the school year." She said with glee, as she began flicking the back of Jake's ear with her index finger. "I want to see your ear turn red with joy from my non stop flicking."

After a few minutes of being flicked upon, Jake got mad. He blurted out "Touch my wenis!"

The teacher stopped the lesson, The whole class turned around in shock and stared at Jake. Mrs. Crumbie looked like she was going to kill someone. Regina stopped flicking.

"Young man!" Mrs. Bigalow shouted, "You apologize immediately!"

"I'm not going to apologize!" Jake shouted back, "Can't you see she's bullying me?" He continued.

"Jake," Mrs. Bigalow said with a threat in her voice, "Either you apologize to Regina and her mother or report to the Principal immediately!"

"Regina and her mother can touch my wenis and so can you for doing nothing about bullying!" Replied Jake.

Mrs. Crumbie was so insulted she withdrew Regina from the school immediately. Mrs. Bigalow called the principal who personally escorted Jake to his office.

"I've called you parents." Principal Stinner told Jake. "Can you give me one good reason why I shouldn't suspend you for one week?"

"Mrs. Bigalow didn't stop Regina from bullying me and I couldn't take it anymore, so I snapped." Jake replied.

"Yes but you cursed and told Regina, her mother, and Mrs. Bigalow to do obscene things to you." Principal Stinner said sternly.

"I didn't curse." Replied Jake confidently.

"You most certainly did young man, you told then to touch your wenis!" Principal Stinner stated.

"There's nothing wrong with that." Jake said, "I do it all the time."

"That's something you are supposed to do privately, Jake, not in public." Principal Stinner said softly.

"I prefer to do it in public because sitting at a desk makes it hurt so much, I have to rub it." Jake replied. "My parents encourage me to do this and even gave me lotion to sooth my aching wenis."

Principal Stinner's face turned red. His eyes bulged. The vein on his forehead looked like it was going to burst. He thought about calling child protective services. He thought about calling the police. He wondered what kind of sick parents taught their kid things like this. Principal Stinner's train of thought was derailed by Jake's question.

"Principal Stinner," Jake asked "What do you think a wenis is?"

"Why it's your male organ Jake, even if you can't pronounce it right." He replied.

"No, Principal Stinner," Jake said, "It's the flap of skin that covers your elbows." He continued. "So you see, it's not my fault."

"What's not your fault Jake?" Principal Stinner inquired.

"That no one at this school knows their own anatomy." He said.

Andy's Problem

Fourteen year old Andy had a big problem. His best friend Bobby had stink breath. He liked Bobby but couldn't stand being near him because every time Bobby opened his mouth, Andy would have to hold his breath so he wouldn't breathe in the toxic fumes coming from Bobby's mouth.

What's worse, Bobby had no idea that his breath was so bad. Bobby was big and mean looking and most kids were afraid to tell him anything negative. Andy had to figure a way to tell Bobby about his stink breath without making Bobby mad.

He thought and thought. Then an idea came to him. Maybe if he put a bottle of minty fresh mouthwash in Bobby's gym locker, with a note written by somebody Bobby didn't know, Bobby might get the hint and start using mouthwash.

Andy got a foreign exchange student Bjorn Bornay to write the note, Bobby didn't know him. Andy told Bjorn to write a note to Bobby telling him he needed to use the mouthwash to make his breath smell nice. Bjorn wrote the note, folded up the paper and handed it to Andy. While Bobby was taking a shower, Andy quickly put the mouthwash and note in Bobby's open locker.

When Bobby came back he saw the mouthwash, mumbled some things about how he liked to get free stuff and opened the note. He read the note, then, got mad, crumpled the note up and slammed it to the floor. He dressed quickly, slammed his locker door shut and stormed out of the locker room. Andy picked up the crumpled note and read it.

It said:

Dear stupid,

You have stink breath that makes the trash bin at high noon smell good. Use this minty fresh mouthwash and spare us all from a fate worse than death, namely standing within 100 feet of you.

Signed,

Someone who can't stand the pain anymore.

Bobby was in a bad mood all that day. He told Andy that he would kill whoever sent him the note and the mouthwash. Andy was worried that Bobby might find out.

Bobby never found out who sent the note. He never found out who sent the mouthwash but he actually started using it. Much to everyone's surprise, using the mouthwash transformed Bobby's nose hair curling, stink breath into minty, nose curling, stink breath. What Andy didn't know was that Bobby's stink breath was caused by a bunch of rotten teeth. He never went to the dentist before he got the mouthwash and he never went to the dentist after he got it so the mouthwash couldn't cure it. Andy's dad got a job in another state a few months later and Andy moved away. He never forgot Bobby. In fact, he was reminded of him every time he passed by a place where there was a sewer backup.

Fitting In

Joey was just entering high school. He was concerned because most of his friends from middle school were going to a different High School Joey didn't know if he would fit in with the new kids he would meet at his new high school. He asked his dad for advice.

Bill, Joey's father was quite popular at his work and literally fit in with any crowd he was in. Bill thought a moment about what he could tell his son. He decided to tell him about the time he came to a realization about the secret to fitting in. This is what Bill told Joey.

When I was a teenager I didn't really fit in anywhere. I knew a lot of people. I had a lot of acquaintances but just a few actual friends. I didn't think of myself as weird but I'm sure there were others at school that did. In fact, one boy, used to pass me by several times a day in my travels around campus. Whenever he passed by he would stop, put his face up to mine and say "You're weird!" Then he would walk away.

I don't recall ever meeting him or seeing him in any of my classes. No one I knew seemed to know him either. I don't know why he thought I was weird or even why he would make it a point to stop and tell me every time he passed by. This went on for some time.

One day, when I was walking home from school a car came barreling down the street at a high rate of speed. As it passed by the part of the sidewalk I was walking on, the driver slammed on his brakes. The car came to a screeching halt and went into reverse and stopped when it was parallel with me. Tinted electric windows on the passenger side rolled down revealing a lone occupant, the driver. It was the boy who always told me I was weird.

When the window rolled down all the way the boy looked me dead in the eye and said "You're weird".

As he proceeded to roll the electric window back up I shouted to him.

I said "I'm glad I'm weird because if everyone was the same the world would be so boring we'd all kill ourselves!"

The boy then rolled the electric window back down, looked at me and replied "You know something; you're not weird after all". Then he rolled the window up and sped off.

I still saw him around campus after that but he never told me I was weird again. He never spoke to me either but at least he didn't call me weird. I don't believe I was actually weird. I don't believe anyone is weird. I think that people are just different. It takes all kinds of people to make the human race and everyone fits in their own way. If you think about it, weird is just a shade in a range of adjectives which included weird, strange different and unique. I prefer unique. The boy in my high school may have been calling me weird but all I was hearing was unique.

The All Time, Epic
Rotten Egg War

Every year, the rich kids at Rob's high school bragged about their annual rotten egg wars on Halloween. Every year they talked about how the poor kids would come up to their exclusive enclave in the hills above them and challenge the rich kids only to be beaten badly by spoiled kids throwing spoiled eggs. The winners of the war got bragging rights for the rest of the school year and the rich kids always got to brag. They bragged mercilessly, taking every opportunity to rub the loss into the poor kids faces.

The rich kids called themselves The Highlanders. They lived up on Mount Aetna , an exclusive development of spacious luxury homes with manicured lawns overlooking the valley where the high school was located. Mount Aetna also overlooked the valley which was dotted with apartment buildings. The high school students who lived in the valley were poor to lower middle class, almost all of them apartment dwellers. These kids were known as Lowlanders.

Martin Luther King High was named after the tireless civil rights leader but it didn'tlive up to the legacy of the great man it was named after. The school was a perfect example to integrated segregation. The school was integrated because the rich and poor both attended classes there. It was, however, segregated in many ways. The school's sports teams included both Highlanders and Lowlanders but the Highlanders occupied the team captain and key positions on the team while the lowlanders occupied the positions that did the grunt work. On the football team, for example, the quarterback, running backs, rushers and kicker were all highlanders.   The lowlanders were mostly in blocking positions, The Highlanders totally controlled student government and with it, student body funds. They were given leadership positions in all of the school's clubs and in classrooms. The Lowlanders just participated.

The Highlanders ruled their enclave. They ran Martin Luther King High School They didn't rule the lowland streets. That honor was reserved for the town's one gang the Hood Rats. Very few Hood Rats were members of the Martin Luther King High student body. The Highlanders made sure that they either dropped out or were kicked out. The Highlanders rarely had to worry about the Hood Rats because most of the time they were in the lowlands they were in their own cars driving to or from somewhere. The Lowlanders worried though, because while the Highlanders could retreat to the relative safety of their own cars, the Lowlanders had to catch the public bus. Hood Rats rode the public bus.

A couple of days before Halloween, Rob talked to his friend Ashton. They both wanted to take bragging rights away from the Highlanders. They were both sick and tired of the Highlander's banter all school year long. Since Ashton had a car and rob didn't, they decided to take Ashton's car. Rob worked at the local supermarket. He found he could get a box of rotten produce for $1.00. They decided rotten produce would be a good counter to the rotten eggs the Highlanders threw on Halloween. They decided to meet up at Rob's house right after school on October 31.

All day long, on October 31, the Highlanders were talking about how they had buried rotten eggs a month before and how those eggs were just laying there, rotting to a fine stink, ready to be dug up and thrown at a Lowlander. They wondered aloud, what Lowlanders would be foolish enough to want to get their clothing and hair permanently "stinkafied" by a ripe, old rotten egg.

Rob met Ashton after school. They went by Robs house to get the boxes of rotten fruit and cartons of "old" eggs. When night fell they drove up to Mt. Aetna . They drove around trying to find where the action was. The streets seemed quiet. As they approached the top of an uphill street, they heard a lot of noise. They decided to park the car and walk over to see if the noise was from an egg battle.

As they reached the top of the street the noise got louder. The hid behind some bushes and peered over the crest of the street towards the downhill side. About halfway down the long street they saw 10 Highlanders engaged in an egg battle with six lowlanders. They realized it was an unfair fight.

Rob and Ashton ran back to Ashton's car. Ashton started the engine. As he cruised to the top of the street, Rob readied the rotten fruit and old eggs. As the car reached the crest of the street, Ashton revved up his engine. He sped downhill at what seemed to be 90 miles per hour. As they passed by the Highlanders, Rob let off a volley of rotten plums, completely surprising the highlanders. He hit 9 of 10 of them. He hit some of the Highlanders on their clothing and others in the head.

When they got to the bottom of the street, Ashton turned around and revved up the engine. He sped back up the hill. This time the Highlanders were ready for them. As Ashton & Rob got close, the Highlanders let off a volley of rotten eggs, christening Ashton's 14 year old car with a fresh coating of slimy stink. Rob returned fire, hitting one especially snotty kid in the forehead with a rotten plum. Two of the Highlanders had a six month old Porsche revved up and waiting to give chase but an exploding rotten watermelon on its windshield stopped them dead. Rob laughed as the Porsche windshield wiper only made his watermelon bomb more thickly coated against the windshield, preventing the car from leaving its parking space.

As soon as the Ashton reached the top of the street, he made an immediate U turn and returned for round three of the Epic battle. As they raced down towards the Highlanders, Rob began throwing rotten peaches at them fast and furious. As the Highlanders clumped together to meet Ashton & Rob's challenge, t he other Lowlanders issued an egg assault from the rear.

Just then, the unmistakable siren of a police squad car blasted. Ashton looked in his rear view mirror and saw the squad car at the top of the street racing towards them. The Highlanders and Lowlanders scattered. Ashton drove up a side street. The squad car bypassed the houses where the battle was happening and turned down the side street Ashton drove down.

Ashton could see them as they turned the corner. Ashton drove down another side street, drove past a few houses and quickly parked the car while simultaneously turning off the lights. Ashton & Rob both ducked down. In a matter of second, the squad car turned the corner and raced past them, not noticing that they were parked. The boys remained ducked down for ten more minutes before Ashton started the car.

As they cruised slowly along the streets, they came to the top of a different street. About half way down they saw a lone Highlander walking casually along the downhill side. Ashton sped up and Rob leaned out the car. He bombed the Highlander with an especially rotten egg he had been saving for a special occasion. As he let the egg fly he yelled "Hood Rat Here" at the top of his lungs.

Rob and Ashton couldn't help but laugh the next day when the Highlanders came to school crying about how the Lowlanders and Hood Rats teamed up, came to their enclave and attacked them. The Highlanders were still jerks but for the rest of the year they didn't brag about their victory in that Halloween's Egg War. Somehow, they seemed to be a little more respectful towards lowlanders and traveled the lowland streets a little less.

Microcosm

Lyrics by The Prophet of Life
As Recorded by The Alternative Rock Band
Teacherz

VERSE 1
The outcasts of the school community
Become the outcasts of society
They live on the fringes
Work in the shadows
Are supported by the underground
Economy

CHORUS
School
Is a microcosm
Of life

VERSE 2
The leaders of the school community
Become the movers and shakers of society
They live in the mansions
They work in the penthouse
Are supported by old boy

Networking
(repeat chorus)

VERSE 3
The average kid in the school community
Becomes a cog in the wheel of society
They live paycheck to paycheck
Work for somebody
They are the backbone of the mainstream
Psychology
(repeat chorus)
BRIDGE
A Glimpse of things to come
Can be reflected in school
But your future depends
On the path you choose

The Kid In The Back of The Class

This could be someone you know:

Did you ever wonder about the kid in the back of the class? The one who rarely talks. The one that may even seem creepy to some. Did you ever wonder what he's thinking about? Did you ever wonder how he feels? He has something to contribute. He has never been given the chance. Do you think he likes being judged as having nothing worthwhile to say?

Yet day after day he just sits there staring blankly but listening intently. You rarely give him a second thought. You assume he is stupid. You treat him like he's a numbskull or even worse, like he doesn't exist at all. Don't you think that he has feelings too?

Would it hurt your reputation, your precious peer ranking to risk sitting next to him one day and trying to talk to him? He may be shy at first but maybe if you got to know him you would find he did have something to offer. Maybe you'd find that he did have a brain and that he had a sense of humor.

But no, you continue to chatter away with your friends. You walk past him on the street like he's a ghost. You go on with your pretty little life. While he is trapped in the back of the room of life, imprisoned in his shyness.

More than Just a Gangster

Roberto Rincon was dead, of that there was no doubt. Vice Principal Barris, the paunchy 63 year old leftover from the old days of law and order in public schools predicted it from the moment he had laid eyes on Roberto just one week earlier. He knew the kid had a record just by looking at him and when he read the anecdotal records on Roberto, it only confirmed his suspicions.

Roberto had been to the Dean's office numerous times for infractions ranging from cursing at teachers, to getting into fights and knocking over campus security when he was fleeing from the Dean. When Dean Sanders grabbing hand startled Roberto, the kid reacted predictably. He turned and swung at the much taller and stockier adult, connected and broke his jaw. That drew Roberto a one year sentence in "Camp" the politically correct name for juvenile prison.

That was before Vice Principal Barris got to Van Buren High. Now Roberto was out of camp and wanted to re-enter the student population at Van Buren. Vice Principal Barris would have never let him return but Principal Nevarrez made the decision. Roberto was waiting by Vice Principal Barris door. His mother left as soon as Principal Nevarrez approved her son's acceptance letter. Vice Principal Barris never even met her.

Now the boy was dead and Vice Principal Barris knew he had to call in the district's Crisis Team. He doubted many kids would grieve over a barely returned gang banger but district protocol determined that he must call in the Crisis Team so that's what he did. Vice Principal Barris hated the "touchy feely" activities utilized by the Crisis Team but as Vice Principal, he was required to be present for all of its sessions.

The Crisis Team arrived at 8:15 a.m. fifteen minutes after school began. They sat idle for the first hour. Shortly after the beginning of second period, campus security brought in four students who refused to go to class. They said they were sad about Roberto. By fourth period there were 20 students in the small conference room where the Crisis Team met. By sixth period, there were so many grieving students; they had to move the Crisis Team to the much larger teacher's cafeteria.

During that day, Vice Principal Barris learned a lot about Roberto. He learned that Roberto lived in the projects that were the main feeder for Van Buren students. He knew that the projects had gang members living in them but he didn't know that a rival gang had been beating up project students that had to walk past their territory to get to Van Buren whether they were gang members or not. He learned that the project gang had been planning retaliation but most of the molested kids thought they were moving too slowly.

Roberto thought so to and one evening he went to a park in the rival gang's territory and waited. In due course, a carload of rival gang members drove by and Roberto pulled a pistol from his waistband and aimed it at the car. He pulled the trigger but the gun jammed. The guys in the car saw him. A shotgun popped out of the back passenger side window and issued a double volley directly at Roberto hitting him in the chest. 15 year old Roberto was killed instantly as the car sped off. A local mother and her four year old daughter standing nearby were also hit but they survived.

For the rest of that week, students and at times, even parents, trickled in to weep and share stories about Roberto. Many students talked about Roberto's great sense of humor and how he frequently went out of his way to help people. A girl who seemed to have a crush on him, wept openly as she said she would miss his smile. A boy said that Roberto was someone you could count on to be there when you needed him.

A mother who had three kids of her own at Van Buren told the Crisis Team the most poignant things about Roberto. She told how Roberto's mother was a party girl who was always on the pill but got pregnant with Roberto once when she had forgotten. She was in her early thirties when she had him. She never really wanted to be a mother and never acted like one. She would often abandon Roberto for days on end. She told the team that Roberto was a Project Child, raised by countless parents and kids who helped feed, clothe and shelter him over the years. She told them how Roberto spent many meals at her table and spent many nights sleeping on her couch.

Everyone in the projects helped to raise money for Roberto's funeral. They had car washes, yard sales and walked around their neighborhood asking for donations. One of the Homies even got his boss at the tee shirt factory to make 100 tee shirts with the words "We'll never forget our Roberto" below a picture of Roberto smiling, at cost ($4.00 each). The kids sold them for $20 each.

The next week the school was closed for spring break. Vice Principal Barris, thought about Roberto that week. He realized that there was more to Roberto than he previously knew. He realized that although Roberto was a gangster, he was still a person who was loyal and made people laugh. He understood why Roberto was loved by so many. It reminded him of something he had heard in church when he was a boy, about how you never know what a profound effect one person can have on the lives of others. He wondered if the neighbors in the projects had raised enough to have a nice funeral for Roberto.

The first day the school returned from spring break, Vice Principal Barris asked one of the students who lived in the projects if they had raised enough for Roberto's funeral. The student told him they had and they had just buried him two days before Spring Break was over. Vice Principal Barris was genuinely pleased to hear that.

As he arrived at his office, he was greeted by an over- weight, middle aged, woman with flaming, bottle red, hair and too much makeup on. She wore old sandals, jeans that were way too tight and a tank top that was far too tiny for a woman of her age and weight. Her gut bulged from beneath the tank top revealing a belly ring. Her two bulbous hands clenched to a stack of textbooks.

She introduced herself as Roberto's mother and told Vice Principal Barris she was there to return his textbooks. She desperately wanted assurance that her returning them would mean that she wouldn't be charged for them. Vice Principal Barris assured her that her returning the books would indeed erase anything that may be owed from their absence. She asked Vice Principal Barris if she could have the photo his secretary took of Roberto when he re-entered school. With a tear in her eye, she admitted that she had no other photos of Roberto and would love to have that one as a memento of her dearly departed son. Vice Principal Barris indicated that he didn't have access to the photo at that moment but could mail it to her in a day or two. She insisted that he email it instead and dashed off her email address on a piece of paper and handed it to him. She apologized and said she had to leave because her new boyfriend was waiting in the car for her and he didn't like to be kept waiting. Then she abruptly left.

Vice Principal Barris walked into his office. He put down the paper and searched his camera's data file for the photo of Roberto. After a few minutes he found it. He uploaded a copy to his district internet account and attached it to an email. His wrinkled but nimble fingers trembled slightly as he typed: "Here is the photo of Roberto you requested, sorry for your loss." As he glanced at the paper Roberto's mother gave him, he was struck by her email address: **miss sexy OG babydoll @ognetwork .com**.

Class Management

Mr. Dow, the Assistant Principal in charge of evaluating teachers entered the Principal's office. "How did your observation of Mr. Blake go today?" The Principal asked.

"I believe Mr. Blake needs to work on improving his classroom management skills." said Mr. Dow.

"Oh," said the Principal, "Why is that?"

"Well, after I was there for just a short time," Mr. Dow said, "I noticed most of the students began throwing paper airplanes all around the room."

"Really," said the Principal, "What was Mr. Blake doing during all this?"

"He was writing a problem on the chalkboard." replied Mr. Dow.

"When I went up to Mr. Blake and informed him of the student's activities, he responded in a way which instantly told me that he needs to improve his classroom management skills?" said Mr. Dow.

"What did he say?" asked the Principal.

"He told me that if I didn't want to get hit, I had better duck." replied Mr. Dow.

When A Teacher Commits Suicide in Their Classroom

It was 8:00 a.m. in the sleepy community of Smalltown, California. A group of students waited for their teacher to open the door to her classroom. As the minutes passed, the door remained closed. The students knew their teacher must be inside because some of them saw her car parked on campus. They asked a teacher from a nearby classroom to let them in the class. He obliged.

Upon entering, they saw their beloved teacher hanging from a light fixture. While the teacher who opened the classroom dialed 911, three students, who couldn't bear to see their teacher hanging, gently lifted her lifeless body as a fourth one cut the rope that held her to the light fixture. They layed it on the floor respectfully. Some students began weeping, others just stared in disbelief. After a short while, paramedics arrived and checked her vitals. They pronounced her dead. Then they carted her body away lake a sack of potatoes.

26 year old Jill Johnson was a popular teacher known as a caring soul. She was always bright and cheerful although the suicide of her father just two years before seemed to trouble her. She even taught a unit on depression for her freshmen recently and told the class that "Suicide was not the answer".

The affected students received counseling. District administrators talked about what a tragedy her death was but no one knows why Ms. Johnson killed herself. Officials weren't 100% sure if she did killed herself as there was no note left at the scene. There were, however, a few things that everyone was sure about. A good teacher was dead. A light in the lives of many children was snuffed out and scores of vulnerable children were devastated. Yet nobody knows why.

The Teacher Who Yelled Too Much

Teachers today have very little in their arsenal to help keep a classroom under control. One of their big guns is yelling. A teacher is definitely not supposed to yell at children but if it is done only on occasion, it can be very effective.

Mr. Dermis was a veteran teacher who had worked at various public high schools in a rough area of a modern major city. He did it for several reasons. For one, he got combat pay (more money for working in a "difficult" area. For another, he wasn't expected to do much teaching, students rarely showed up to his class and administrators almost never came in. They were just happy to have an employee who showed up consistently.

In the middle of the school year, Mr. Dermis was transferred to a school on the slightly more affluent East side of town. He figured it would be business as usual. He didn't understand why most of the students showed up to his class every day. What's worse, they wanted to learn something. Lacking good teaching skills, Mr. Dermis went to Plan B, he lectured a lot. He figured it would be easy. He would talk and the students would listen. He taught history, so whenever he didn't know something, he made stuff up. What did it matter, the students weren't alive during the Civil War, how would they know what happened?

Mr. Dermis act didn't fare well at the new school. On his first day, most of his students listened attentively to his lecture but a few grew bored about the middle of the one hour class. A couple of students began talking. Mr. Dermis began yelling at them. They quieted down immediately. As the weeks wore on however, yelling at the kids became Mr. Dermis go to plan. The students in his class became increasingly rowdy and as they did, Mr. Dermis yelling became more frequent and less effective.

Mr. Dermis classroom was held on the second floor on the inner side of a horseshoe shaped building. It overlooked a beautiful courtyard with flowers and shrubs surrounding a stately winding cement walkway with beautiful stone benches interspersed. For the 75 years that the school had existed the walkway had always been a tranquil setting where students could study or eat lunch and where employees could sit quietly and recharge their batteries on their break.

Mr. Dermis always kept his windows open. He preferred fresh air to the artificial atmosphere created by central air. Within a month of Mr. Dermis arriving, it became commonplace for the tranquility of the walkway to be disturbed by Mr. Dermis frequent yelling and something occasionally flying out of his window to the walkway below. By the middle of the first semester, administration visits to Mr. Dermis class became increasingly frequent. Mr. Dermis was told that he was expected to actually teach and to stop making things up.

Mr. Dermis actually tried to improve his teaching. He started watching The History Channel and reading books about the periods of history he was actually teaching. He still had a problem with the rowdiness of the students and he still used yelling a lot to try and control them. The students caught on to the stuff he made up before and they lost respect for him. Mr. Dermis was having one heck of a semester at his new East side high school.

Mr. Dermis could often be seen in the faculty lounge on his conference period and on his lunch break. He often looked weary and dejected. One Monday morning Mr. Pierce, a physics teacher at the school, noticed that Mr. Dermis was actually excited. He had an old cobweb filled record player which he was cleaning with a damp cloth. Mr. Pierce approached Mr. Dermis and asked why he seemed so excited.

Mr. Dermis relayed that he would be covering The Great Depression this week and that he found an old record that could help the students understand The Great Depression. Mr. Pierce carried on with his day and towards the last period, he happened to be walking the winding sidewalk in the courtyard below Mr. Dermis classroom. He could hear Mr. Dermis talking about The Great Depression and then he heard a needle touching upon a vinyl record. He heard a guitar playing and then he heard "Hobo Joe, Hobo Joe, He was a hobo." Then he heard Mr. Dermis yelling and saw the record player come flying out of Mr. Dermis window and crashing onto the pavement below.

Cafeteria Food

Lyrics by The Prophet of Life
As recorded by the Alternative Rock Band
Teacherz
Verse 1
Is that pizza
We're having today?
Why's the pepperoni
Turning gray?
The Chicken A La King
Looks regurgitated
Has this place been
Board of Health rated?

CHORUS 1
Cafeteria food
Rotten, disgusting,
Half Baked and crude
Puts you in
An institutional mood
Makes you nauseas
Makes you rude
We all hate cafeteria food!

VERSE 2
The milk and juice
Expired last week
They mash the potatoes
With their feet
The oatmeal is hard
The cornbread falls apart
The spaghetti is moving
Call the national guard!
CHORUS 1
Cafeteria food
Rotten, disgusting,
Half Baked and crude
Puts you in
An institutional mood
Makes you nauseas
Makes you rude
We all hate cafeteria food !

The Key Ring

Mr. Sherman was a great teacher, there was no doubt about that. He was dedicated and popular with the students. He coached the school's Baseball team after school. Mr. Sherman had been at Eisenhower High School for many years and over the years, he had acquired many keys on his Faculty key ring.

Mr. Mc Nulty remembered back when he first began at Eisenhower, and he inherited a key ring full of keys he never used. He turned all but three of them back into the main office. Mr. Sherman yelled at Mr. McNulty when he heard about it.

"Are you crazy?" He shouted, "You never give back keys, keys are a measure of your status on campus. Keys are your power!"

Now, it was ten years later and Mr. Mc Nulty was the Teacher Union Representative for the school. One day, a replacement teacher came to his room and told him he had to go to the Vice Principal's office on Union business. When he got there he was greeted by Mr. Beedy, an ambitious, young Vice Principal.

Mr. Mc Nulty knew Mr. Beedy for three years. When he first came to Eisenhower under Principal Gipson, he was the low administrator on the totem pole and as a result he kept a low profile. He used to ask Mc Nulty to help him write memos because he was unsure of himself. Last year, however, Gipson was replaced with Mr. Jessup. Mr. Jessup was a Vice Principal at Mills High along with Mr. Beedy. Now Beedy went from being a bottom feeder to being The Principal's right hand man.

"I am calling you out of courtesy." Beedy told Mc Nulty abruptly, with a nervous timber in his voice. "This is already a done deal but Mr. Sherman suggested I tell you about it before I proceed."

"Okay," Said Mc Nulty.

"Head Custodian Atkins was making his rounds this morning and found two students standing by a door with a teacher's key ring. He grabbed the key ring and brought the students to my office. After interviewing them, they told me that they were putting away some equipment for Mr. Sherman." Mr. Beedy Explained.

"So Mr. Sherman used poor judgement in handing the keys to students and left them unattended." Stated Mr. Mc Nulty.

"Oh, it gets worse", Beedy replied. "Upon examining the key ring I found about a dozen forged keys and you, know, Mr. Mc Nulty, that forging district keys is more than just a violation of district policy, it's a crime."

"What did you do Mr. Beedy?" Mc Nulty said slowly and deliberately as anger filled his eyes.

"Why, I called Mr. Sherman to my office, had a school policeman waiting with me and told him I was going to have him fired, arrested and have him taken out in handcuffs in the middle of lunch. Mr. Beedy said nervously. "But Mr. Sherman told me that I had better run it past you before I do anything." He continued.

"Well it's a good thing you did." Said Mr. Mc Nulty. "Because you would have made the biggest mistake of your career if you had done that!" He continued.

"How do you figure?" Mr. Beedy asked.

"All of the district keys say Do Not Duplicate, correct?" Asked Mr. Mc Nulty

"Correct." Replied Mr. Beedy

"And you know that Locksmiths won't duplicate district keys because they are aware it is a crime correct?" Said Mc Nulty.

"I suppose." Replied Mr. Beedy.

"Then how was Mr. Sherman able to duplicate the keys on his key ring?"Mr. Mc Nulty asked.

"He could have…"Mr. Beedy replied sheepishly.

"Are you saying that Mr. Sherman has a key duplicating kit at home?" Quipped   Mr. Mc Nulty angrily.

"Well, I'm not saying that…" Mr. Beedy Replied.

"Mr. Beedy, if you are going to have Mr. Sherman arrested, you better have irrefutable proof that he dupilcated those keys." Mr. Mc Nulty Stated. "Otherwise you will be opening up this school and this district to a gigantic law suit." He Continued.

Mr. Beedy thought for a minute. As he thought he kept trying to start to tell Mr. Mc Nulty points he had but he never got past saying single words like but or if which were followed by him shaking his head. Finally, he pursed his lips as if he was going to say something profound.

"If I don't have an arrest or a firing, what do I have?" Mr. Beedy asked.

"You have a letter of reprimand for poor judgement in giving school property to students and leaving them unattended." Mr. Mc Nulty replied.

As a result of the meeting, Mr. Sherman got a letter of reprimand. He wasn't fired or arrested. He wasn't paraded in handcuffs in front of the students who he was popular with and the school and district avoided a lawsuit. Mr. Sherman, still popular continued to teach and coach at Eisenhower for many more years. Mr. Mc Nulty continued being the Union Rep.

As for Mr. Beedy, he avoided making what would have been a career ending mistake. He was promoted to Principal of another school a year later. He was fired for incompetence two years after that, when he tried a similar tactic at the school he was Principal at and there was no one with the wisdom and foresight of Mr. Mc Nulty to counsel or stop him.

Grades Are Due

Lyrics by The Prophet of Life

As recorded by the Alternative Rock Band
Teacherz

VERSE 1

You've been playing around
Having your fun
Your class work's neglected
Your homework's undone
All of a sudden
Up it pops
Teacher's revenge
You're heart stops

CHORUS

Grades are due
The burden is on you
To bring up your grades
Better do it quick before it's too late

VERSE 2

Make up the assignments
Study all day and night
Got to give it your all

For this to come out right

Turn off the tele
Unplug the phone
You got yourself into this mess
Gotta get out of it alone

CHORUS
Grades are due
The burden is on you
To bring up your grades
Before it's too late
Grades are due!

Corruption, Scandal and Resignation
at The School District Controlled by A Group of Billionaires

I'm going to tell you a story about a school district I have been following. It's a good sized district in the Western United States. For the past decade it has been struggling to wrest control away from a group of billionaires who have decided to spend money buying school board elections. The School Board races for this district are among the most expensive in the nation almost always costing millions of dollars to win a seat that pays about $50,000 a year.

A few years ago, the billionaires were able to put a Superintendent in place that would do their bidding in a big way. He called himself a Doctor but he got a doctorate with 9 units of work instead of the normal 45. He actively advocated spending a billion dollars to buy computers for the district using funds earmarked for improving buildings, while holding stock in the computer company. He also appeared to have given that company preferential status in the bidding for the billion dollar contract. When the local press grumbled about that, he sold the stock but its uncertain if he sold it outright at a tidy profit or if he sold it to a "friend" for $1 with the thought of buying it back at some advantageous point in the future.

This industrious Superintendent also hired a slew of outside contractors to solve a lot of district problems. He "improved" an already well functioning district attendance and record keeping system with a "New" more expensive one that never quite did what it was supposed to. He took a sex scandal at one school and turned it into a district witch hunt where he put teachers in district jail for being accused of anything by anybody. He also advocated and sponsored laws at the state level to instantly fire teachers for merely being accused of any wrongdoing without due process.

A typical example is a teachers put in teacher jail is a teacher who failed two students. The students accused him of hitting them in front of a class full of students. When school administrators interviewed the class full of "witnesses" none of them saw the teacher hitting anyone.. One of his two accusers retracted her statement and told an administrator that she and other student made up the story to get the teacher fired because he failed them. The teacher was cleared by the school administration but when the mother of the accusing student who didn't recant her story showed up at a meeting with a Assistant Superintendent and complained, the teacher was put in teacher jail.

That Superintendent resigned. The School Board members who's elections were paid for by the billionaires and who collaborated with him are still in power. They brought in the guy that this Superintendent replaced as an interim Superintendent. The Superintendent who was replaced, was forced to resign because he was being paid $100.000 a year extra as a "consultant" to a book company that the district buys books from. He was also accused to sexually harassing an employee who worked under him. The district still named a school after him. As soon as he took power again, another sexually harassment suit against him surfaced. Until the School Board members who collaborated with the corruption of the resigning Superintendent are replaced, the corruption will not end with his departure.

Kindly Mr. Bluster

Mr. Bluster was a kindly, roly poly, gentile, elderly man who taught special students at a public middle school. Mr. Burns saw him in the mornings before school as they both arrived at school 90 minutes early every day. Mr. Bluster was always very friendly. He said hello to everyone he passed when walking in the halls. His students all commented on how nice he was.

Mr. Burns hadn't been absent in over 17 years. As the semester wore on, he noticed that Mr. Bluster, while new to the school had also been there every day. That impressed Mr. Burns. He meant to tell Mr. Bluster how impressed he was with his excellent attendance but the amount of work involved in being a teacher always got in the way and he often forgot, not remembering until he was already on his way home from work.

Then one day, Mr. Bluster was absent. Then he was absent the next. When Mr. Bluster was absent a third day in a row, Mr. Burns began to worry. On the fourth day Mr. Bluster returned. Mr. Burns walked right up to him first thing in the morning, expressed his concern and asked why Mr. Bluster had been out for three days in a row.

"I had to have some reconstructive surgery on my jaw." Mr. Bluster replied.

"Reconstructive surgery, are you sure you've has enough time to heal?" Mr. Burns retorted.

"Yes, I'm fine." Mr. Buster stated. "I just needed a final surgery on my jaw, just a couple of teeth this time." He continued.

"How many reconstructive surgeries have you had on your jaw?" Queried Mr. Burns.

"Seven." Replied Mr. Bluster.

"What happened?" Asked Mr. Burns.

Mr. Bluster's face became sallow and his face sank sadly as he began to tell his story.

"About five years ago, I was walking to my car in the parking lot of a shopping center and four teenage boys jumped me. One of them hit me in the face with a baseball bat. My jaw was broken and had to be put back together over several surgeries." Mr. Bluster explained.

"Wow!" Mr. Burns exclaimed. "Poor fellow, you must have been in a lot of pain." He stated sympathetically.

A sudden gleam in his eye changed Mr. Buster's sad expression to one of animation.

"I was in severe pain when I regained consciousness after being out for a few seconds. I came to and saw the four boys standing a few feet away going through my grocery bags and wallet. I also saw that they had abandoned the baseball bat. I noticed that it was within my reach. Filled with pain, I reached over, picked up the bat and staggered towards the four boys." He said.

"So the boys run away?" Mr. Burns asked.

"They tried to," replied Mr. Bluster but I caught them and I beat the crap out of them! I beat them, I beat them! I beat the crap out of them!"

"Wow!" replied Mr. Burns. "Did the police charge you with anything?"

"I don't know," replied Mr. Bluster. "I picked up my wallet, my money and my groceries. Then, I went to my car and drove away.

Just Another Day At The Office

Hiram Whitmore High School was named after a Colonel in the Union Army during the American Civil War. The school was one of the first established in the community which at the time it was established, some eighty years previous, was an upper middle class neighborhood. As times changed, the original population died off and most of their children had long since moved out to the suburbs, the neighborhood surrounding Whitmore High also changed. The once grand houses were disheveled by years of neglect from the lower middle class and poor people who lived in them. Poverty, crime and the blight of drug addiction all became commonplace.

Once a model of excellence in education, Whitmore won many academic awards and had high standings among the nation's educational institutions during and even after the time the upper middle class walked its hallowed halls. Sometime after the mid 1970's the school began to lose its luster and although there were a few stellar scholars every year, it became synonymous with other cesspools of public education and was commonly referred to as "Witless High".

Mister Wilson knew exactly how he ended up at Hiram Whitmore High School. He had just been hired by the district when he was offered the job as an English teacher at Whitmore. He immediately took it, mostly because, he didn't know any better. The school was in a rough neighborhood filled with violent students and a lackluster faculty.

He got to work about a half an hour early this Tuesday, in the seventeenth week of the fourth year in his teaching career. He entered the faculty lounge to the tomes of Ms. Bitters complaining about Johnny Rockisaw spitting into her purse in a knee jerk reaction to an F she gave him on a still life he drew. The students called her "The Nazi" Ms. Bitters held her students to the highest of standards, expected them to follow in lock step to her commands and yelled at and ridiculed them mercilessly when they didn't. She was only nice to them when administrators came by to observe her class, kind of like how the Nazi's were nice to the POW's when the Red Cross representatives came to visit the POW camps.

Suddenly Ms. Bozono came walking into the lounge. Ms Bozono was appropriately named. She was in her mid fifties, tall, very thin and unlike most women, she was going bald. Her baldness was concentrated in the middle of her scalp. To compensate, she kept her hair on the sides extremely long. She styled her hair in a perm so her hair literally looked like Bozo the clown. Already having burned through three marriages and divorces, Ms. Bozono was always on the prowl for husband number four. Ms. Bozono spoke loudly: "I'm looking for me a husband." The six male faculty members in the lounge simultaneously realized it was almost time for class, so they ran out of the room in a great hurry.

As he walked to his classroom, Mr. Payoso approached him. Mr. Payoso, the school's Vice Principal, was a burly serio-comic type of man. He was often gentle but had a violent temper which occasionally flared up. Mr. Payoso was at Whitmore because he punched a student who was in the midst of attacking him. The district couldn't fire him, because he was acting in self defense but district policy dictated that employees being assaulted and battered should just smile and take it. District Officials moved Mr. Payoso to Whitmore as punishment for protecting himself.

"Wilson", I have a budget for you to sign, can you come to my office after 1st period." Said Mr. Payoso.

Wilson was also the union rep, a thankless job no one else wanted, and so he had to sign off on all of the school's budgets.

"Uh, Okay." Wilson uttered in response.

During first period, Mr. Wilson had the students read "The Amigo Brothers", a story about boxing and friendship. He tried to stress how friendship was an important theme in the story. He likened the friendship in Amigo Brothers to the friendship between Heavyweight boxers Joe Louis and Max Schmeling. Louis defeated Schmeling whose victories boxing victories in the mid 1930's were used as propaganda by Nazi Germany at a time when they were promoting Aryan superiority. The two men became lifelong friends after the fight. Unfortunately, Wilson's analogy was lost on the students who had never heard of Joe Louis, let alone Max Schmeling.

The next period, second period was Wilson's prep period. As soon as class was over, Wilson went to Mr. Payoso's office. Mr. Payoso motioned for him to come in and handed him a budget form. Wilson looked it over and found something unsettling.

"It says here that you are using funds from a 5500 account for text books." Wilson stated.

"Yeah, Mr. Bikini needed some textbooks for his algebra 2 class." Mr. Payoso responded.

"It is my understanding that 5500 is a building fund. Isn't that the money needed to buy desks for the new bungalows?" Wilson stated.

"Yes, but this was an emergency and I couldn't find money elsewhere." Mr. Payoso interjected. Just then, Ms. Bozono burst into the room crying hysterically. Mr. Payoso scowled.

"What's wrong Ms. Bozono?" asked Wilson.

"My Masters Thesis!" she exclaimed. "I gave it to my assistant to copy and he lost it." She continued.

"Let me get this straight…" Mr. Payoso stated with flared nostrils indicating anger, "You used a District Copy Machine to copy your personal crap!" He concluded.

Ms. Bozono's facial expression changed from one of sad distress to extreme anger.

"Shove it Payoso, you big, dumb, payaso! I just lost six months of work due to the incompetence of your school staff! I don't need this crap! I'm finishing my Masters in Administration and looking for me a husband. I quit!"

Then she stormed off and left the school, never to return.

Since Ms Bozono's class was next to Mr. Wilsons and Wilson didn't have a class that period, Mr. Payoso sent Wilson to cover Ms. Bozono's class for the rest of the period.

Although her class was next door Wilson had never even entered Ms. Bozono's class before. All he knew was that it was usually noisy and there was periodic pounding on the wall. Now, there was a group of students standing out in front of the class waiting for their teacher to open the door.

Wilson opened the door and was greeted by a strange sight. There were various sizes and colors of construction paper stacked up and strewn about the room. The walls and even ceiling were covered with letters. Not words, just alphabetical letters haphazardly stapled everywhere. A short, plump, female student approached Wilson.

"Are we going to read a book today?" she inquired hopefully.

"Of course, this is an English class." Wilson replied. "Why, what do you usually do in here?" He asked.

'That crazy lady just has us cut out paper letters and staple them to the walls." The girl replied.

The period passed quickly as Wilson had Ms. Bozono's class read The Amigo Brothers. They seemed to really enjoy doing some work for a change.

Wilson realized that Ms. Bozono was possibly the worst teacher he had encountered since Mrs. Gluton. He covered Ms. Gluton's class several times his first month at Whitmore. She frequently called in sick and always had the same lesson plan. It always said have students read page 87 and answer questions 1-6. It was frustrating for both the students and whoever had to sub for her or cover her class. About a week after the last time Wilson covered her class, the FBI came and arrested her for welfare scams. She had put the names and social security numbers of about 30 of her students from 10 different families and put all of their addresses as her home address with different apartment numbers even though Mrs. Glutton lived in a house, and there were no apartments. The arrest came unexpectedly and Ms. Glutton left her brand new Cadillac parked on the Whitmore campus. By the time it was towed way three days later, it was full of scratches and dents, the windows were broken and wheels removed.

The next period went by quickly making way for lunch. Wilson stood in line in the teacher's cafeteria, which oddly enough, served that same food as the student cafeteria at triple the price. Wilson resigned himself to settling down with a chalupa and a soggy salad. Just as he paid for his meal Mr. Payoso cut in front of the remaining teachers in line. He led Mrs. Poolay by the hand. He told the cafeteria worked to serve Mrs. Poolay and told Mrs. Pollay he would give her a letter of reprimand next time he caught her standing in the student line trying to get her food for the lower price. Mrs. Pollay simply asked how much soup was and when told it was a dollar, ordered soup in her thick French accent.

Wilson suffered through his sub standard lunch and left the cafeteria. Fourth and fifth period went surprisingly well. Sixth period, the last of the day, he heard an awful lot of noise coming from Ms. Bozono's class. He opened the door that adjoined his room and Ms. Bozonos. He immediately noticed the lights were off. He saw several students making and throwing paper airplanes at each other. A couple of students were playing a game called wrestle mania. Mrs. Poolay was sitting in the dark reading a newspaper. He felt sorry for Mrs. Poolay. She was an 83 year old retired teacher who had to come out of retirement because she lost most of her pension in the stock market crash of 2008. She was a bit senile and couldn't really handle the students but needed the money to pay her rent. He wondered what would happen to Mrs. Poolay if she didn't have this job. Mrs. Poolay reminded Wilson of Ms. Mc Ginny.

Mrs. Mc Ginny was a teacher who worked at Whitmore long past her prime. She was old, senile and cantankerous. Most of her students were failing her classes because she lost most of assignments they turned into her. She would often sit and just stare at the walls. Her students, understandably bored, took to destroying her classroom. They etched graffiti not only onto her desks and walls but her floorboards. They even took out the keys on her computer keyboard and put them back in backwards. Ms. Mc Ginny retired way too late. She had lots of money but no relatives to take care of her or to check in on her once in a while. All she had was her little Chihuahua Tinkerbell. She retired in June, and died in her paid up condominium in October of the same year. Her body wasn't found until March of the following year, the skeleton of a Chihuahua cuddled up by her side.

He looked in on Mrs. Poolay a little later. The students were doing what they were before but Mrs. Poolay was sitting at her desk with a waste basket over her head. Wilson removed the waste basket, and settled the class down. Later she screamed for Wilson to help her. He opened the door to find that a female student had arranged all of the desks in the shape of a runway culminating at Mrs. Poolay's desk. The student was walking on top of them and was about to step on Mrs. Poolay's head when Wilson opened the door and told her to get down and take her seat.

The students all listened to Wilson. He had no problems with discipline. It wasn't like that his first year, He would turn his head to write the answer to a question he had pre-written on the whiteboard and 23 pieces of balled up paper would fly towards his head. The third week of his second year however, something happened to change all of that. A student he had bonded with was arrested for trying to sell cocaine to an undercover cop. Out on bail, the 17 year old thought he would be going away for 20 years. He jumped the fence to the school and walked into Wilson's class. He opened up his gym bag, pulled out a pistol and put it up to Wilson's forehead.

"What are you going to do now Mister?" The kid said mockingly.

Wilson knew that the kid wouldn't pull the trigger on the only teacher he had bonded with.

"Pull the trigger" Wilson dared him.

The kid just laughed, put the gun back in the gym bag and left the class. Wilson never pressed charges against the kid. The police cocaine case fell through and the kid ended up getting a job as a supervisor at a warehouse when he was 19. He made more money than Wilson.

Since that day, Wilson never had any problems with discipline. The word of the incident spread through the student gossip mill. Wilson was thought of as the crazy teacher who stared down the barrel of a gun and told the student wielding it to pull the trigger. The students figured if he was macho enough to do that, what would he do to unarmed students if he got mad. If he ever did get upset, all he had to do was raise his voice just a little bit and he was met with instant compliance.

Quelling rebellions in the class next door aside, the rest of sixth period passed by quickly. When the day was over, Wilson signed out, and left the main building leaving the Vice Principal's budget unsigned. As he drove home, he thought of his colleagues he had encountered that day. He thought about others as well.

He thought about the Counselor who used to sleep all day and was busted on the popular TV show 60 Minutes, for his night time activities of being the President of a "college", a diploma mill whose degrees, all paid for with hard money, were completely worthless. He thought of the Math teacher who was living with a 15 year old student and who was fired not because the girl's parents complained but because her grandparents complained He thought about the social studies teacher who quit to become a police officer, the science teacher who was committed after having a mental breakdown at a faculty meeting and the first year teacher who quit because he couldn't stand being incompetent. He remembered them all and wondered how he ended up in such a circus. In the back of his mind he harbored the suspicion that perhaps he fit right in.

Teenage Mysteries of Life Solved.

You know how your parents are always telling you not to do things, but they never tell you why? They tell you things like work hard, get good grades, respect others, be careful of the company you keep and stay away from drugs and alcohol. All your mysteries are about to be solved. This article is going to tell you why.

Parents tell you to work hard and get good grades because, for most societies across the globe, school is the path to upward mobility. Even the poorest of people from the poorest of families can move upward economically, socially and intellectually by getting a good education. Going to a good school can help you develop into a more disciplined, well versed, well rounded person. Going to the right school could get you powerful connections that will help you advance in the future. People without money or connections can get into the right school but only through excellent grades. Graduating will be the key to a good job. A good job is the key to economic advancement.

Parents tell you to respect others. They tell you this because people who don't respect others don't get respect themselves. If you get a job and don't show your colleagues and customers respect you won't have a job for long. Gangsters and criminals don't get respect. They think they do but what they actually get is fake respect to their faces while people are laughing at them behind their back. This is because they have no job and no future. They don't respect anyone. They give intimidation through fear and have to carry a weapon to get the fear. That's pretty sad.

Parents tell you to be careful of the company you keep. This is because you are judged by the company you keep. If you hang around with the brainiacs, people think you are one of them. People will think you are smart. If you hang around people who curse a lot, you will end up cussing a lot. If you hang around thugs, people think you are a thug or a wanna be thug. When thugs are attacked by rivals guess who else suffers the consequences? You do. While the thugs have other thugs for backup, you've got nobody. If thugs commit crimes, and you hang with them you automatically become a suspect. Suspects can sometimes be arrested ad even charged with a crime. Even if you aren't convicted, you may still get a reputation. One that may follow you into your adult life.

Parents tell you to stay away from drugs and alcohol. This is because drugs and alcohol are addictive. They can become the focus of your life while everything else, including more important things fall by the wayside. It's difficult to concentrate in school when you are high. If you can't concentrate, you can't pass classes. If you can't pass classes, you can't graduate. If you don't graduate, you can't get a decent job. Before you know it, you will be in the workforce. If you are high all the time you won't be able to keep a job. If you already have a reputation and even a nick name that indicates you are a druggie, it's likely that it will follow you into the world of work. Who is going to hire a drug addict?

There are reasons that your parents tell you these things. They may not tell you. Perhaps they don't know how to tell you. The reasons may not be clear to them but the reasons are clear and they make logical sense. They are all based on caring. Your parents care about your future. They only want the best for you. They have lived longer than you and have more experiences with life than you do. They have learned from their own mistakes or from the mistakes of their friends. They may see you making some of the same mistakes and they are trying to save you the aggravation of suffering the consequences of those mistakes.

Who Will Teach Our Children?

Teaching was once a well-respected profession in America. The hours were long, the work was hard and the students didn't always show their respect. At least there was job security. People went into teaching to make a difference, to help build the future and to have a profession that they could be proud of and retire from.

Now, older, good, professional teachers are being forced to retire early. Younger, newer, good, professional teachers are being laid off. Many of them spent years of their lives getting an AA, a BA and one or more teaching credentials. Some even got a masters or worked hard to become national board certified before either being laid off or leaving to find a more secure profession due to constant annual threats of being laid off.

The Charter Movement has put pressure on an already financially struggling public education system and replaced public schools with charter schools that pay teachers even less than public schools. Teacher turnover in charter schools is extremely high even higher than in public schools.

Kids in college, who have a choice can choose to pick an insecure, low paying job as a teacher or pick an insecure corporate job at three times the starting salary. Enrollment in Teacher Colleges across America is down 75%. Is it any wonder why enrollment in education as a major is so low in universities? Within 5-10 years we will begin to see headlines like "Who Will Teach Our Children?

School districts have tried convincing people with degrees in engineering to teach math or science. Many of them, however, have few teaching skills and often can't control the student that are in their charge. School districts try and import teachers from third world nations. Many of them soon realize that they have gone from a culture of respect for teachers to one of student empowerment. The ones who are good get little chance to succeed, as students file complaints against them because they cannot understand them due to their thick accents.

In time, teaching may well change from a profession to a place people who are out of work gravitate towards until something better comes along. These people will not have the commitment to the profession or to our students that someone who is in it for a career has. They will just be in it for a paycheck. With the best and brightest choosing other professions, who will teach our children?

Hap Wilson

Hap Wilson was always a happy child. He laughed and played. He chased after butterflies and, when he got near them, he held out his index finger and they landed on it. As they walked up his finger to its tip he gave them butterfly kisses by batting his eyelashes.

As hap got older, he began to face the demands of school, and getting along with other children, some of which hated him for no reason that he could figure. One child in particular, Harry Winkwater, made his school life unbearable. Harry bullied Hap every chance he got. Harry would often take the desert or even main course from Hap's school lunch. He would verbally make fun of Hap at every opportunity. Several times during every class, Harry would go up behind Hap and flick his index finger behind the tips of Hap's big ears.

Hap's teachers all turned a blind eye to the bullying. His father told him to fight back and stand up for himself. His mother talked to Harry's mother in an attempt to get her to make him stop. That seemed to work for a while but once Harry was off punishment, he returned to bullying Hap with a vengeance.

Over the years, as the bullying continued, Hap began to change. He was not the happy, fun living boy he used to be. He became a depressed, hopeless boy who often felt suicidal. Then one day, he was sent to live with his mother's sister, his Aunt Frannie. Life at Aunt Frannie's home was very different. He went to a school without bullies. It was a school where he was accepted and actually made friends.

Hap Thrived in that environment. He excelled in school, sports and even took karate classes. He became a black belt in just three short years.

Hap lived with Aunt Frannie during his middle school years. When it was time to return for high school, Hap, as agreed, was to go back to live with his parents. Afraid of going back, Hap confided his fears to Aunt Frannie. He told her about Harry Winkwater and his endless bullying.

Aunt Frannie told him that he was a different person now, than he was when he was bullied. She told him that there was a chance that Harry Winkwater wouldn't even be going to the high school he was going to. She told him that if he was confronted by Harry Winkwater or any bully, he should not fight back, but merely move out of the way of the bully's punches, forcing them to expend their own energy. This way, he could beat the bully without ever laying a hand on him. Finally, Aunt Frannie told Hap that the Harry Winkwaters of the world rarely amounted to anything and that he, as a better person should show Harry some compassion.

Hap returned and went to high school that fall. Sure enough, Harry Winkwater was there sitting behind him in his first period class. Just when he least expected it, Harry flicked his index finger behind the tip of Hap's left eat.

"Welcome back old friend!" Harry whispered sarcastically.

For the next two minutes, Hap wasn't listening to the teacher's lecture. He was listening intently to Harry's movements. Then he heard Harry's jacket rumbling.

He knew Harry was about to flick his finger behind Hap's left ear again. With lighting speed, Hap lifted his textbook with his left hand and placed it behind his left ear. The book reached Hap's ear just as Harry was releasing his index finger. Harry gave the textbook a hard flick.

"Ouch!" Harry shouted while pulling his gnarled finger away.

The whole class looked at Harry. By this time, Hap's book was back on his desk because he returned it with the same lightning speed he had lifted it up to his ear with.

"Is there a problem Mr. Winkwater?" The teacher asked sternly.

"No problem sir." Harry replied while rubbing his injured finger.

The next day, Harry came to school with a splint on his finger. Harry didn't bother Hap again. Hap didn't really pay attention to Harry. As the months passed, Hap went on with his life and did well in school. One night, a friend of his suggested they go bowling. Hap hadn't been bowling in quite a while, so he agreed.

While Hap was choosing a bowling ball, he noticed a commotion at one of the lane tables. He heard a boy shouting "Harry, will you please stop!" He looked over and saw Harry flicking his index finger on the tip another boy's ear. It didn't occur to Hap that when Harry stopped picking on him he would find someone else to bully. Then a girl got between Harry and the boy. Harry Seemed upset that her body was preventing him from engaging in his ear flicking pleasure.

The, the girl shouted at the top of her lungs. "Harry Winkwater is a stupid cow kisser!"

Everyone in the bowling alley turned around and stared at Harry, the girl and the male bullying victim. Harry lifted his hand to give the girl a backhanded slap. Hap stepped up, grabbed Harry's hand and bent it back until Harry had to get on his knees and follow it to avoid the pain of it being bent back.

"Now, Harry, I'm sure you are a better man than that. You would never actually hit a young woman would you?" Hap said.

"Of course not, I was only funning." Harry replied. "In fact, if you let me go, I'll apologize to the girl." He continued.

Hap released Harry and stepped back. Harry sprung to his feet.

"Okay, you Piss Ant." Harry Shouted. "You're not at school with administrators and teachers to protect you!" He continued

Harry charged forward, throwing punches. Hap, following Aunt Frannie's advice, merely moved out of the way.

"Oh, running away huh punk?" Harry Shouted. "I Knew you weren't about anything. Now I'm gonna kick your scaredy cat little ass!" He said as he charged forward.

As Harry advanced, he threw a barrage of punches but none of the made contact because Hap kept evading them. After a few barrages Harry's frustration built to a climax.

"C'mon Damn it! Stop running, kick my ass, if you can." Harry Shouted.

"I don't have to." Hap replied. "You're doing a pretty good job of kicking your own ass."

After a few more barrages without connecting Harry became tired out.

"I quit!" Harry Declared. "I can't fight someone who won't fight back." He concluded.

"But you can sure pick on them can't you?" Said Hap.

"What did you say?" Harry inquired

"I said, you sure know how to pick on people that won't fight back." But that's not going to happen anymore is it Harry?"

"No, why not?" Harry replied.

Because I'm here now and if I hear of you picking on anyone, you're going to have to deal with me." Hap replied.

"And…What are you going to do?" asked Harry with a tinge of fear in his voice.
"I'm going to have to make you kick your own ass again." Harry concluded.

And so ended the bullying career of Harry Winkwater.

Over the years, Harry began to replace bullying with studying. He turned out to be pretty smart. He eventually became a psychologist and worked for an organization that helped both the victims and perpetrators of bullying. I guess it takes a bully to know a bully and Harry made one hell of a good healer for everyone involved in the bullying cycle.

Hap, had a good life. He graduated college, got a good job and married his high school sweetheart, who turned out to be the girl Harry was about to slap at the bowling alley. Harry and Hap actually became good friends. Hap was truly a happy man. And sometimes, when nobody was looking, he would chase butterflies and hold out his index finger. When they climbed up to the top, he would bat his eyelashes and give them a butterfly kiss.

Mr. Happyhands New Lesson

Mr. Happyhands had been teaching U.S. Government at Bell High for at least 20 years. Happyhands wasn't his real last name. It was the name the students gave him.

Since the beginning of his career, he would begin writing the key information he wanted students to know about a set of pages in a chapter on the chalkboard on the left hand side of his room. After he completed the writing on that chalkboard, he would spend a few minutes lecturing about it. Then he would begin writing on the next chalk board and when he was finished, he would lecture on that one. The procedure would repeat itself until he filled up all seven of the chalkboards in his classroom.

Students in his class were expected to copy the material on all seven chalkboards and listen to his lecture. Many students complained about getting writer's cramp but Mr. Happyhands never seemed to have any problems with writing because the next period, he would erase all seven chalkboards and begin again. He did this five periods a day, five days a week, nine months a year for 19 years.

Then last year the school Principal told him he had to stop teaching that way. The Principal told him the old ways of teaching were no good. He told Mr. Happyhands that he would have to follow the new method teachers in

his school were trying. A method that was more self-directed for the students.

Over the next few months, Mr. Happyhands began changing his style of teaching. Instead of having the students copy off of his seven chalk boards, he typed out a series of questions that guided students towards the key information in each chapter in the textbook. The students seemed to like the new method better. Now, instead of getting complaints about writer's cramp, he got complaints about brain freeze.

One morning in late November, Mr. Happyhands handed out an assignment.

"I've got good news and bad news for you students, which do you want to hear first.?" He said.

"Let's hear the bad news!" One student suggested.

"I have 25 questions for you to answer today!" He said to a chorus of moans from the student desks.

"The good news…" He said. "Is that all of the answers are on just four pages 331-334." He continued.

He went to his desk to take roll. When he finished he looked over his class. Several of the students were on their cell phones. A few had their
heads down and appeared to be napping. Several others were talking quietly in small groups. Only two of the students were reading their texts and answering the 25 questions. Mr. Happyhands wondered how participation in his class had deteriorated to this sorry state. The first week of the semester, every student brought their book to class. By the tenth week about half of the students brought their books. At least with half the class having a book, students could pair up and answer his questions. Now, in the 17th week of a 20 week semester it was down to two students brining their book! He decided to do something about it.

He began asking the students where their books were. Most of the students left their books at home, some left them in their school lockers and some left them in other classrooms. A few said they lost their textbook. Mr. Happyhands realized that this new method of self-directed teaching allowed the students to direct themselves not to participate by choosing not to bring the textbook to class. The majority of his students didn't have the one thing in the world that could answer the questions they were assigned to answer.

"Students, let's suspend using the textbook today." He said.

The students looked at Mr. Happyhands oddly.

"What are we going to do?" Asked one student.

"How about I write a summary of the key points on the board and you copy them and use those key points to answer the questions?" He said.

"Okay!" Shouted the majority of students.

What about us?" Asked the two students working out of their textbooks.

"Well…" Mr. Happyhands replied. "Since you guys already started answering your questions, you two can continue answering the questions that way." He continued.

Then Mr, Happyhands began writing. He began on the chalkboard on the left hand side of his classroom. All of the students broke out their notebooks and pens and began copying. Forty five minutes and seven chalkboards later he finished. Several of the students were scribbling away, several of them were finishing.

"Mr., there are just four minutes left in the period. When are we supposed to answer the 25 questions?" She asked.

"I guess you will all have to answer them for homework." He said as the two students who brought their books to class handed him their completed assignments.

"So, class, what was the real lesson today?" Mr. Happyhands asked triumphantly.

"Bring you textbook to class!" responded several of the students in unison.

I Don't Have Time

As Recorded by
The Alternative Rock Band Teacherz
Hear it at New Ideas at Bandcamp.com

Verse 1

Too many students
Too few breaks
Work just piles up
And slowly takes
A toll
On my soul

Too much pressure
Too much stress
The clock is ticking
On the best
Years
Of our lives

Chorus A
I don't have time
For your interruptions
I don't have time
For your obstructions

Vague instructions
For your staff reductions
I don't have tim3

Verse 2
Too few Indians
Too many chiefs
Too much manipulation
By the thieves
Who steal
From the public till

Too many panaceas
But no real cure
Us caught in the middle
Having to endure
This crap
It's time to fight back

Chorus B

I don't have time
For your rash conclusions
I don't have time
For orchestrated confusion

Half baked solutions
For your grand delusions
I don't have time

The Bushwhacker

He first met Elmo Santana about the third week of school. He was registered into Mr. Blevin's class but had not shown up before then. When Mr. Blevins asked why he hadn't come to school the prior three weeks Elmo replied "Cause I'm The Bushwhacker!"

After a few weeks, Mr. Blevins got a better picture of Elmo. He was smart, but shifty. He was always scheming to get something. Sometimes it was a loophole that would yield a better grade, other times, he would lie to try and get over on a girl and still other times, he was extorting money from other students.

One day, Elmo blatantly threatened another student in front of Mr. Blevins. Mr. Blevins sent Elmo down to the dean's office with a note entitled "*Physical Threat*". The dean sent Elmo back a half an hour later with a note that said "*Counseled*". Mr. Blevins was angry but he didn't show his anger in front of the students. He accepted Elmo back into his class, tried to engage him in the day's lesson and waited until after school As he entered the class, Mr. Blevins could have sworn he heard Elmo mumbling "You'll never get the Bushwhacker." under his breath.

Mr. Blevins went to the dean's office after school. He wanted to know why the dean did nothing more than counsel Elmo. The dean told him that unless there was a credible threat, district policy prevented him from going beyond counseling.

The next day, the boy who Elmo threatened came in with a black eye. Mr. Blevins immediately had him escorted to the Dean's Office. The dean sent the boy back about twenty minutes later. He sent Mr. Blevins a note explaining that Juan told him he got the black eye in an after school game of football. When the bell rang at the end of the period, Elmo remained afterwards. He walked up to Mr. Blevins.

"Why did you send Juan to the dean's office today?" He asked.

"You know why Elmo, because you threatened Juan yesterday and today he came in with a black eye." Said Mr. Blevins firmly.

"Hey!" Stated Elmo boldly. "Stop getting into my business cause you'll never get the Bushwhacker. The Bushwhacker is too smart for you!"

Several weeks went by. Elmo kept getting into trouble. Mr. Blevins continued to send him down to the dean. The dean kept sending him back. Mr. Blevins continued to have conversations with the dean about why more wasn't being done about Elmo.

Then, one day, Elmo didn't come to class. Mr. Blevins thought it was odd but he welcomed the relief of not having to put up with The Bushwhacker's drama.

Then, two more days passed and still, Elmo didn't come to class. By the fourth day Mr. Blevins began to wonder why. He went to the Dean's office and told the dean he thought Elmo was ditching his class. The dean told Mr. Blevins that Elmo got into a fight and was kicked out of school.

As the semester rolled along, Mr. Blevins enjoyed teaching his class. No one seemed to talk about Elmo any more. Then, one day, Mr. Blevins overheard a student mention Elmo. The boy was telling another student that Elmo's brother was killed in a drive-by shooting.

A few weeks later Mr. Blevins went to a restaurant near school on his lunch break. He entered the restaurant and there, sitting at a table was Elmo. Mr. Blevins decided to talk to him.

"Hi, Elmo, I heard you are not at our school anymore. How do you like your new school?" Mr. Blevins asked nervously.

"I'm 18, so I dropped out." Replied Elmo.

"Elmo, I know we haven't been the best of friends…" Mr. Blevins stated.

"But I was sorry to hear about your brother." He continued.

'That's okay Mister, what goes around comes around." Elmo replied.

A few more weeks passed. The semester was winding down. Mr. Blevins was preparing for final exams in a couple of weeks. He was starting to review with the students. Then, one day he saw Elmo at the same restaurant. Elmo sat pensively, sipping a soda. Mr. Blevins noticed he had the tattoo of a teardrop next to one of his eyes. Mr. Blevins knew that tattoo was only given when a gangster murdered someone.

"Hi Elmo." Mr. Blevins said. "How are things?"

"Not so good Mister." Elmo replied.

"Oh," said Mr. Blevins. "Why?"

"I shot at the guy who shot my brother but I missed." He said. "I got his brother instead. He shot back at me but he missed. You know no one gets the Bushwhacker Mister. I'll get him next time though." He concluded.

Mr. Blevins didn't know what to say in reply. How could someone reply to that? Mr. Blevins just walked away. That was the last time he saw Elmo. A couple of days later he overheard two students talking about him. One kid said he heard gunshots in front of his apartment building and saw a car crash into a parked car. Another kid said he went down to the car and recognized his friend, the Bushwhacker, slumped over the steering wheel moaning. He said the police showed up but refused to allow an ambulance past the police line until Elmo expired.

Mr. Blevins thought about a quote he once hear "He who lives by the sword shall die by the sword." He knew that The Bushwhacker wasn't the nicest person. He knew that he had murdered someone. But, did he deserve to die at 18 years of

age? He knew that he wasn't born The Bushwhacker. He was born Elmo Santana. The Bushwhacker was made, created on the mean streets of Southeast Los Angeles.

He knew that somewhere inside of The Bushwhacker was a kid named Elmo who never got to realize his potential. Finally, Mr. Blevins wondered why he lived in a world where kids killed each other to make a name for themselves through violence instead of trying to make a name for themselves as artists or writers or scholars. Then, Mr. Blevins had to change gears and put thoughts of the Bushwhacker behind him because he had a series of Final exams to give.

The Good Guy

Ralph Castaneda was at the top of his class. He got straight A's and passed his state exams with flying colors. The day the State Exam results came in his name was read over the schools loudspeaker as having a perfect score in all subjects. Normally shy and retiring, Ralph was slightly embarrassed when he heard his name.

The bell rang and Ralph left his 3rd period class and began walking to his 4th period. As he walked, Harold Brewster, a classmate of his began shouting at him.

"Ralph, you think you're a good guy don't you?" He shouted. Ralph ignored him.

A few seconds later, Harold repeated, "Ralph, you think you're a good guy don't you?"

"I don't think I'm good, I know I'm good." Ralph replied.

Harold, who wanted to impress some friends he was walking with, retorted: "I'm Better!"

As soon as the words left Harold's lips, Ralph issued a lightning fast reply. "Why? Were you sick?"

Corporal Punishment

Eight year old Julian knew the Principal would be coming for him. He was engaged in a water balloon was with his best friend Tim. After getting hit several times, Julian was hell bent on vengeance.

Julian filled up four water balloons and chased after Tim. Tim was much faster than Julian. He easily ran away from him. Julian lobbed the first water balloon, it passed 10 feet over Tim head and splattered onto the ground about 20 feet in front of Tim. He threw a second one right after that but it was further away from Tim than the first one had been.

Julian decided to hold onto his last two water balloons and chase after Tim until Tim got tired and slowed down. Julian knew that he could outlast Tim because what he lacked in speed, he made up for in stamina. After four minutes, Tim got tired and began slowing down. Julian pulled within 15 feet of Tim. He lobbed one more water balloon. It hit Tim in the arm but bounced off, not breaking until it hit the ground about six feet from Tim's left side.

Tim ran into the Main Building. He jogged down the hall. Julian was closing in behind him. Julian became oblivious to the other people in the hallway. He was fixated upon Tim and only Tim. He was within five feet of time. Tim turned a corner. Julian followed close after him as if drawn by a magnetic pull. As he rounded the corner he was within two feet of Tim. He sped up in an attempt to smash the water balloon on Tim's head.

Tim swerved to the side. Instead of smashing the water balloon on Tim's head, Julian ended up smashing it on Mrs. Featherweight's large back. The ironically named Mrs. Featherweight, was the school's 400 pound janitor.

Shocked, both boys ran away as fast as their little legs could carry them. Tim wasn't sure if Mrs. Featherweight saw him. Julian, however, was pretty sure Mrs. Featherweight new it was he who hit her with the water balloon. He wasn't sure if she saw him but she lived down the street from him all of his life and he thought that she might recognize the sound his feet made when he ran.

The bell signifying the end of lunch rang. Julian went back to his class. He thought the Principal would come right away. After 45 minutes the principal still didn't come to get him. Julian thought perhaps Mrs. Featherweight didn't recognize the sound of his footsteps after all. After an hour, Julian began to think he had actually gotten away with the accidental water bombing. Then the Principal's Voice came over the class loudspeaker.

"Please send Julian Sandz to my office." The Principal said.

Julian's teacher excused him. He began walking slowly down the hallway towards The Principal's Office. He walked slowly deliberately and with dread of what horror awaited him behind the door of the Principal's Office. Julian knew he was going to be in pain in a few minutes. He lived in a place where corporal punishment was totally legal. Parents regularly spanked their children when they were bad. School administrators also had the power to spank the naughty children.

They were not allowed to remove their clothing or touch their bodies directly but they could swat or paddle them through their clothing.

Mrs. Mc Ginty, the Principal of Julian's school was a spanker. She had a gigantic, square, wooden paddle with holes in it. She would have the misbehaving student bend over and touch their toes. Then she would take the big paddle in her hand and with a dramatic flair, would lift the paddle high above her head bringing it down squarely on the student's bottom. The holes paddle would make a loud whooshing sound as the paddle was dropping. This increased the tension for the student because they could hear the instrument of their pain coming before they actually felt the pain of the blow.

Julian walked at a snail's pace, trying to think of a way to get out of the pending spanking. He could stop at the drinking fountain, throw some water on the floor and slip, pretending he was badly hurt and leave in an ambulance. He could just run away and join the circus. He could deny everything and ask to call his lawyer. In reality, Julian knew those were all lame ideas. He didn't think an injury would soften Mrs. McGinty's heart. He knew the circus wouldn't take him and he had no lawyer. Suddenly, he got an idea!

Julian stopped off in the boys' bathroom. He went into one of the stalls. He removed two rolls of toilet paper, unzipped his pants and put a roll down his pants behind each butt cheek. Then Julian walked over to the Principal's Office with some pep in his step. He entered the office with confidence. Principal Mc Ginty looked at Julian Sternly. Then she spoke.

"I understand that you threw a water bomb at our Mrs. Featherweight." She said sternly.

"It was an accident Miss." Replied Julian.

"So you are not denying that you did it?" Said Mrs. Mc Ginty.

"No miss, I am not denying that I did it, I am only denying that it was intentional." Replied Julian.

"Are you mocking me?" Principal Mc Ginty said.

"No miss, mocking you would be He changes his voice to a high pitched shrillness) "I'm Principal Mc Ginty, I like spankings!"

Anger filled Principal Mc Ginty's eyes. Julian almost thought he saw steam coming out of her ears like in an old cartoon. She picked up her paddle.

"Bend over and touch your toes!" Principal Mc Ginty yelled in an angry tone.
"Two swats for you, one for water bombing poor Mrs. Featherweight and a second for mocking me!" She said.

Julian complied. He could hear the whoosh of the paddle as it sailed through the air. He felt a slight concussion of it hitting his padded bottom. Julian wasn't in pain, so he didn't make a sound. Shocked, that Julian hadn't uttered a sound, Principal Mc Ginty thought she wasn't swatting him hard enough. She raised the paddle almost to the ceiling. The wind whistling through the paddle made the whooshing sound even more loudly than before. This time when it hit Julian did say something.

"That felt good, can you do it again? " He said with gusto.

Principal Mc Ginty became even angrier. She began paddling his bottom like a woman possessed and began swatting his bottom over and over again. Each time he felt a swat hit his bottom, Julian would make a snide comment like: oh the joy! or are you liking this as much as I am Miss Happy Spanker?" After a dozen swats Principal Mc Ginty began to see scraps of toilet paper fly out of Julian's pants. The sight of the toilet paper somehow brought Principal mc Ginty to her senses. She realized that Julian had stuffed toilet paper down his pants. She realized that she had gotten carried away with spanking him. She also knew that she could not legally remove the toilet paper from his pants. She also knew that she could not legally remove the toilet paper from his pants.

Mrs. Mc Ginny's demeanor totally changed. She told Julian to sit down. She knew what he had done. She knew, that he knew, that she knew. She also knew, that he knew, she couldn't do anything about it. She decided to take a different approach to Julian.

"So, Julian, I see that you have stuffed toilet paper down your pants. You think you are smart don't you?" Said Principal Mc Ginty

"I don't think, I know!" Replied Julian defiantly.

"And what would you have done if I had continued swatting you until the toilet paper shreaded and I was wailing on your bottom?" She asked

"I would file child abuse charges against you." Julian replied.

"Okay, Julian, let's come to an understanding." Principal Mc Ginty said. "I will agree to never swat you again as long as you agree to never tell anyone about stuffing toilet paper down your pants."

"Okay, I agree with that." Said Julian.

Over the next two years, Julian was called into the Principal's Office a couple of times but he was never again swatted. True to his word, Julian never told anyone about stuffing toilet paper down his pants before the swatting.

The French Substitute

Mr. Donner was going to be out sick that day. He made it clear to Alma, his teaching assistant, that he did call for a substitute teacher to replace him. Mrs. Du Daux (Pronounce doo dah) showed up promptly at 8:00 A.M. She was a thin, fair skinned woman of about 90. She wore a royal blue felt pencil skirt and a royal blue felt coat and hat. Her wispy, curly, auburn hair, poked out from beneath her hat.

Mrs Du Daux immediately asked Alma for the day's lesson plans. Her piercing blue eyes looked them over.

"What is your name dear?" She asked Alma in a thick French accent.

"Alma Madam." Replied Alma.

"Remember dear, your job is to support me. Do whatever I ask of you and we shall get along just fine." Mrs. Du Daux said sternly.

Then she looked over the class. There were about 40 teenagers. Some students were studying. Most students, however, were either listening to music on ipads or texting on their cell phones. A few were playing video games. Mrs. Du Daux clapped her hands four times rapidly. Most of the students stopped what they were doing and looked up at her. Then, she introduced herself to the class.

"Good morning Children!" She said cheerfully.

As soon as the word children escaped her lips, there was grumbling among the students. Some of them began to make comments. It was obvious that Mrs. Du Dux had made a bad first impression.

"Children?" Said one student. "Don't she know we in high school?!" She continued.

"My name is Mrs. Du Daux." She continued.

"Doo Dah!" Said one student.

"Yo, grandma, is you famous?" Said another student.

"Didn't they name a parade after you?" Said a third student.

"No children!" Exclaimed Mrs. Du Daux. "My name is spelled D-u, D-a-u-x and pronounced doo dah!"

"Doo Dah." Replied a student. "Like that old song: Camp Town races sing a song doo dah, doo dah!"

"No child," Mrs. Du Daux replied. "Not like that song."

"Did they write that song about you?" Asked another student.

"That song is over 100 years old." Replied Mrs. Du Daux.

"And your point is…?" Replied a student

"I am only 83 years old!" Replied Mrs. Du Daux.

"Only!!!" one student replied while most of the other students laughed.

The look on Mrs. Du Daux changed from one of lighthearted conversational engagement to stern, quiet, anger.

"The assignment is written on the board. Kindly follow the directions and turn in your papers at the end of the period." Mrs. Du Daux told the class.

Then Mrs. Du Daux, calmly walked over to the teacher's desk. Opened her purse, got out a newspaper, opened it up and began reading the classified ads. The period went by slowly but Mr. Donner left an easy lesson so most of the students were able to complete it without any help. The next period, Mrs. Du Daux just said "I am your teacher for today" instead of giving her name. That period she also directed the students to follow the directions on the board and read her newspaper.

When lunch time came, Mrs. Du Daux walked quickly to the cafeteria. She told the serving lady "I only have one dollar to spend, give me a bowl soup!"

"I'm sorry madam." Said the serving lady. "Soup is $1.50 a cup. $2.25 if you want a bowl."

"I can only spend $1.00. Can you give me a bowl and give me credit for the rest?" She asked.

The serving lady pointed to a sign that read: "Credit will only be extended to adults at least 85 years of age when accompanied by both parents."

"Very well," Said Mrs. Du Daux, "Give me a bowl." She continued as she handed the serving lady a five dollar bill.

Alma overheard Mrs. Du Daux telling another teacher that she had to come out of retirement at her age because her 47 year old son moved back in with her and she couldn't afford to support the both of them on her pension. She said that she hated working as a substitute but that was all she could find although she searched the want ads every day for a permanent teaching position.

Mrs Du Daux kept on introducing the lesson and then reading her newspaper for the rest of the day. The last period of the day, one student, Reyna, asked

Mrs. Du Daux to help her with the lesson. Mrs. Du Daux just ignored her and kept on reading her newspaper. Alma sat with Reyna and helped her with the class work.

About 45 minutes later they completed the work. Reyna began rearranging the student work tables. Each rectangular work table was about five feet long and two and one half feet wide. She arranged them like an elevated sidewalk from the wall near the door to the teacher's desk.

"I'll teach you to ignore me you doo dah head!" Said Reyna.

Then she hoisted herself on top of the work table farthest from Mrs. Du Daux's desk. She began walking towards Mrs. Du Daux. As she began to walk she yelled.

"You ignored me, so now I'm going to step on your head!"

Mrs. Du Daux lowered her newspaper. Seeing the young girl briskly walking towards her, Mrs. Du Daux panicked. She turned to Alma.

"Help Alma, Help Me!" She screamed in a high pitched voice.

Reyna kept walking. Just as she was about to reach the desk Alma spoke.

"Get down off of the work table Reyna!" She said sternly.

"Yes miss." Reyna replied. Then she got down from the table.

Shortly after that, the dismissal bell rang. As soon as it did Mrs. Du Daux sprinted out of the classroom before the kids could get out of their chairs. Alma closed up the classroom. She made sure the doors were locked. Then she walked towards the main office to sign out.

On her way to sign out she saw Mrs. Du Daux pulling away in a 1993 Chevy Malibu. The old car belched black smoke as it sputtered down the street. Her windows were rolled down and her radio was blasting. "And now a great old song by Steven Foster…" Said the announcer. As a band began playing a familiar old tune, a singer began to sing "Camp Town races sing this song Doo Dah, Doo Dah…!"

Alma wondered how desperate someone would have to be to come out of retirement at 83 years of age to work at a job they didn't really like. She felt sorry for Mrs. Du Daux but she felt sorrier for the students that she was assigned to teach that day. She wanted to tell the Principal how bad the French substitute was but she thought it wasn't her place. Besides, she wasn't sure if Mrs. Du Daux always taught that way or if she shut down as a result of being flustered by the student's rude comments and put downs. After all, she began the day with a lot of energy and enthusiasm but it seemed to drain out of her after a few minutes of abuse by the students.

Mrs. Du Daux seemed to be from another era. An era where teachers dressed up and students automatically showed them respect because they were teachers. She thought about how one needs to have a thick skin to be a teacher nowadays. She wondered how things changed and when they changed. She wondered what kind of teacher she would. She also wondered if she should perhaps revisit her decision to become a teacher in the first place.

High School

A Song by Alternative Rock Band Teacherz
Hear it at New Ideas on Bandcamp.com

VERSE 1

He's no dope
He just smokes it
That is why
Johnny can't focus
Johnny can't read
Johnny can't write
But he can put up
One hell of a fight

He used to be hooked on phonics
Now he's acutely hooked on chronic

CHORUS 1

High School
He goes to high school
He used to be cool
Now he's a fool
As his dreams go up
In a puff of smoke

VERSE 2

She was the queen
Of the cheerleading scene
With the passion & drive
To succeed
She began using speed
To get ahead
Then she began
To lose her edge

In a world of beggars, she was a chooser
Now she's just a coked out loser

CHORUS 2

She goes to High School
High School
She used to be "in"
Now she's just thin
As her future goes
Up her nose

VERSE 3

They're selling drugs on our campuses
It seems like a nationwide epidemic
Why they do it anin't exactly clear
We'll think on it while we down
Another beer
And another beer
And another beer
And still another beer

They go to High School
High School
High School
High School

The Big Drug Bust

Mr. Bravo and Mr. Harris were Deans at a high school in a rough, inner-city neighborhood. The school had its own resident probation officer and two resident police officers. Once a week, the local police department sent a police officer with a drug sniffing dog as part of the school district's Drug Abatement Program.

In keeping with district policy, the deans randomly selected a classroom for the dog to be led into. Mr. Bravo and Harris entered the classroom with the local police officer and dog in tow. Mr. Harris then spoke.

"Good day. Please put both of your hands on top of the desk." He stated as he waited until all of the student's complied.

"Today, as part of the district's Drug Abatement Program, this classroom was randomly selected to be visited by a specially trained police dog. At this time, I want you all to leave your backpack and all of your belongings where they are and walk outside with Dean Bravo." He continued.

The students cooperated. When dean Bravo led them outside, they saw the two school police officers, one male and one female, awaiting them. The students were lined up and Dean Bravo and one of the officers searched their pockets while the other officer watched them to insure no one tried to discard anything or pass anything off to another student.

Meanwhile, inside of the classroom, the officer let the drug sniffing dog off of his leash. The dog ran around the room sniffing various backpacks. Then the dog, a black European Shepard, dug its nose into one particular backpack. It sniffed furiously and began wagging its tale and barking loudly.

The local police officer brought the backpack over to an empty student desk. He unzipped the main compartment and gently emptied its contents onto the desk top. He carefully examined the contents. Two blue 9" by 7" composition books, a one inch pencil sharpener, an X-Men comic book, a shoe lace, a single wrapped, Crustable brand peanut butter and jelly sandwich. The officer checked the other pockets on the backpack. One pocket was completely empty. The other had 2 pencils, 3 pens, a 2" bright pink eraser, and a used toothbrush.

The officer then sniffed the inside of the main compartment of the backpack. He could instantly detect the pungent odor of a type of marijuana known as "Kush". There was nothing inside of the backpack, no buds, no stems, no seeds that could be associated with that odor. The students that were led outside and searched returned. The student who owned the backpack had nothing illegal or even unusual in his pockets.

Harris led the officer with the dog out of the classroom. As they left the classroom, the dogs began to get anxious. They let the dog lead them where it wanted to go. It walked down the hallway. About 30 feet all from the classroom, the dog began sniffing wildly at a particular group of lockers.

Dean Harris pulled out his locker keys. He opened the first locker in the group. It was empty. He opened the second locker in the group. It had two textbooks and a notebook in it. He opened the third locker in the group. It was jammed with textbooks. On top of the textbooks was a small scale and a quart size zip-lock bag full of Kush.

Dean Harris went back to the Dean's office to check the school records to find out which student was assigned to that locker.

Dean Bravo escorted the boy who owned the Kush smelling backpack to the Dean's Office for questioning. After a few questions, Dean Bravo found out that the boy's name was Juan. He also discovered that Juan kept his backpack in the same locker where the scale and zip-lock bag of Kush were found.

Meanwhile, Dean Harris found the boy who owned the locker (Ralph) and escorted him to the Dean's Office. When questioned, Ralph stated that he shared the locker with six other students. He gave Dean Harris the name of the students that shared the locker. Since the Deans already talked to Juan and Ralph, the other four boys who shared the locker were escorted to the Dean's office for questioning.

The first two boys of the remaining four told Dean Harris that they were just students and had nothing to do with the Kush & scale. Their stories checked out, they had no discipline problems and good grades. They declined to give Dean Harris any information about the other students who shared the locker.

Dean Bravo interviewed the first of the remaining two boys. His name was Cisco. Cisco had poor grades and discipline problems. He was well known to both deans. Dean Bravo asked Cisco for his cell phone. Dean Bravo looked through it. He came upon a video. The video was of a room with a table in the middle of it. As the camera panned towards the table, a stack of money and baggies of marijuana could be seen. Cisco's voice could be overheard stating "This is what we've got to do to survive."

Dean Bravo put Cisco in Dean Harris office. He went to get the last boy who shared the locker. His name was Joe. Joe didn't have any discipline problems other than being stopped while in the company of a couple of school thugs. His grades were not spectacular but were not bad. He had a C-average. Dean Bravo questioned him but he refused to say anything. After getting nowhere questioning Joe for about twenty minutes Dean Bravo called in School Police Officer Young. Officer Young also questioned Joe but Joe still refused to speak.

Meanwhile, Cisco was telling a very interesting story in Dean Harris' office. He told Dean Harris that Dean Bravo had already decided that he was the one who would be charged for the marijuana due to the incriminating video on his cell phone. Cisco told Dean Harris that he was being wrongfully accused and the Joe, who was in Dean Bravo's office actually owned the Kush. In fact, he said, the video was taken at Joe's house because Joe has a bunch of weed plants in his backyard.

Dean Harris picked up the phone and called Dean Bravo's office. When dean Bravo answered, Dean Harris told him what Cisco had said. Dean Bravo told Dean Harris to send the student in his office back to class. Dean Harris sent Cisco back to class. A few minutes later, Dean Bravo dropped Joe off in Dean Harris' office. Dean Bravo told Dean Harris that he and Officer Young were going to lunch and asked Dean Harris to keep an eye on Joe until they returned.

Dean Bravo and Officer Young got into Officer Young's patrol car and left campus. They went straight to Joe's house. When they arrived, there was a middle aged, overweight woman sitting on the porch.

"Excuse me madam, are you Joe Reynado's mother?" Asked Officer Young.

"Si, I am Claudia Reynado, I am his mother." Replied the woman.

"Can we talk to you a minute?" Asked Officer Young.

"Sure." Replied Sra. Reynado.

"Your son is having some trouble at school." Said Dean Bravo. "It involves a video, is it all right if we come in and look around your home?" He continued.

"Why you wanna do that?" Sra Reynado asked.

"We want to see if your son is actually in possession of the things on the video." Said Officer Young. "He might be falsely accused and we be able to determine that he is not in possession of the things in the video which would discredit his accuser." He continued.

"Sure". Replied Sra Reynado.

The two men walked through the home. They glanced around the living room. They walked through the kitchen, glancing at counter tops and glancing in cabinets that were already opened. They entered a bedroom. On the wall was a poster from the movie Scarface. There was also the table from the video with large stacks of cash and several dozen baggies filled with Kush.

They entered the backyard and saw rows of marijuana plants of various heights. There was a shed behind the plants. They entered that and found lots of marijuana in various forms of drying and packaging. Officer Young called the local police department. They sent several squad cars and vans.

Within three hours they had tallied $3,486.00 in cash and 27 pounds of marijuana in various stages of being gown or processed. It would become the biggest drug bust in the history of the school district. Joe was arrested and released the same day. The Dean and the Principal of the high school pressed for an expulsion of the student but the school district just moved him to another school while he was awaiting trial.

The fact that he and Dean Harris were involved in a record breaking drug bust was not what Dean Bravo considered the most memorable event of the entire incident. The most memorable event was Sra Reynado's reply to a question Dean Bravo asked her as the police were confiscating the money and marijuana from her home.

When Dean Bravo asked Sra Reynado what she thought her son was doing with all of that marijuana she gave an unusual answer.

"My son had nothing. He was not interested in anything. I tried to get him involved in school but he didn't care. I tried to get him involved in sports and he didn't care about that either. For many years, he had bad grades and just sat around the house watching TV. Thjen, a family friend gave him some seeds. He planted them and they began to grow. He really took good care of those plants. He finally cared about something. Marijuana? I don't know from no stinking marijuana, I only know that I was happy because finally, my Joe had found something he cared about!"

A Tale of Two Brothers

This is a tale of twin brothers, Rob and Bob. They were as different as night and day. They went to the same high school and were in all of the same classes together. They both were average students. Bob knew his classes were challenging and his teachers were excellent. He knew that the rigorous coursework was preparing him for college. He was proud of the grades he earned even if they weren't A's. He was delighted with the grades on his report card. Rob felt shame when he got his grades. He knew he was brilliant and was angry that he got C's. He blamed his grades on crappy teaching.

When it came to extra curricular activities, Bob was eager to help out with fund raisers, school dances, pep rallies and anything involving the school community or community service. His positive attitude made him popular with teachers and other students. Rob was indifferent towards helping out with anything. He did help out sometimes but his poor attitude and constant complaining made people avoid asking him to participate in things. When-ever the boys were presented with a challenge in class or for an extra curricular activity, Bob was always excited to meet the challenge as an opportunity to grow. Rob was almost always bored and looked at challenges as obstacles that cut into his video game playing time.

Both Bob and Rob graduated from high school. Both Bob and Rob applied to college. Since Bob had a lot of extra-curricular activities and letters of recommendation, he felt joy when he got accepted to five different colleges and could choose the one he wanted to go to. Since Rob had few extra-curricular activities and no letters of recommendation, he felt sadness when he was rejected by the colleges he really wanted to go to and was waitlisted by a mediocre college. Bob began college the autumn after he graduated high school. Rob didn't begin college until the next school year.

Bob was aptly named. He rolled with the things that life sent his way. Like a buoy he literally bobbed up and down in the waters of life and kept afloat during its many storms. Rob was also aptly named. He felt life owed him. He always felt like he got a bad deal from life. He always felt like he had been robbed. The difference between the twins came down to one word, attitude. The way they saw obstacles, the impressions they made upon others and even their success in life came down to their attitude towards life. So the question is, dear reader, which of the twins are you? Are you a Bob or a Rob?

I'm Taking Roll

A Song by Alternative Rock Band Teacherz

Hear it on New Ideas on Bandcamp.com

PA Announcement:

Good Morning teachers,

This is Mr. Wimpy

You may now begin taking roll

Please be advised that there were

 A lot of absences yesterday due to

the big ditching party

Please do not allow students into

your class without an absence slip !

Verse 1

Pounding in my head

Caffine in my veins

Don't contribute to my pain

Thunder in my heart

Lightning in my soul

Shut up, I'm taking roll !

Chorus

I'm taking roll

I'm taking roll

I'm taking roll

Shut up !

PA2   Sorry for the interruption,
Students, there are an awful lot of you
 standing over by the noodle machine this morning
Remember, noodle machine is not an official class

Verse 2
Why are you late?
Where's your absence slip?
I don't have time for lame excuses
Who's that making noise?
When are you going to learn?
Oh no, here comes my heartburn
(repeat chorus, jam)

PA3.   Teachers, there a rather large
 fire has broken out in a trash can
in the lunch area and the fire alarm
 isn't working again
Any teacher with a conference this period
should report there immediately.
Please bring a trash can filled with water.

The Power of The Pen

One day Maria came to class early and handed Mr. Burnside a handwritten letter on school notebook paper and asked him to look it over. It was a letter of apology. Mr. Burnside read the letter. Filled with grammatical errors and misspelled curse words, it told the story of a little girl who refused to eat a slice of pizza because she was nauseas. It told about a Church Deacon who then, dropped the slice of pizza onto the floor and told the little girl to eat it. It told about a brave little girl who defied the Deacon and was told to not dare come back to church until she wrote him a letter of apology.

"Why are you writing this letter?" Mr. Burnside asked.

"Because I haven't been back to my church in three months and I want to go back today." She replied.

"Do you go with your family?" He asked.

"No, a bus comes to our neighborhood and picks a bunch of children up." She Replied.

"What do you want to do with this letter?" Mr. Burnside asked Maria.

"I want to give it to the Deacon." She said with a hint of anger in her voice.

"Do you mind it I help you rewrite the letter?" H asked.

"Sure." She said sheepishly.

For the next half hour Mr. Burnside helped Maria take out the curse words and correct the grammar in the letter. Then he asked her if he could type the letter so that it would look nice. Maria agreed. Mr. Burnside typed the letter and then gave it to her.

"I have one other correction Maria." He said as he handed Maria the freshly typed letter. "Give this to the Pastor of your church instead of the Deacon."

Maria took the letter. Mr. Burnside knew she would give it to her Pastor. He was interested to see what would happen as a result. The next day, when Maria came to class, Mr. Burnside asked her what happened at church.

Maria told Mr. Burnside that when she got off of the bus and walked up the steps to the church the Deacon was waiting for her. He refused to let Maria enter until she gave him a letter of apology. Maria got in an argument with the Deacon. The argument got so loud that the Pastor had to intervene. When he did the deacon told him that Maria couldn't return to church until she gave him a letter of apology. The Pastor asked Maria if that were true. Maria just smiled and handed the Pastor the neatly typed letter.

"My teacher told me to give my letter of apology to you." She said as she handed him the letter.

The Pastor read the letter. Then he handed it to the Deacon. The Deacon read it.

"Is this true?" The Pastor asked the Deacon.

"Of course not, I would never tell a child anything like that." The Deacon Said.

"Would you like to ask any of the 35 children that saw what happened Pastor?" Asked Maria.

Then the Deacon admitted to the version of events that was in Marias letter. He was fired on the spot.

Mr. Burnside listened to the story and was glad to hear that Maria's letter got results.

"Maria, have you ever heard the saying "The pen is mightier than the sword?"

"Yes." Replied Maria.

"Your letter, is an example of the power of the pen." He said.

The Letter Maria wrote, the one that got results appears below:

Dear Pastor,

My name is Maria I am writing to apologize for my behavior the last time I went to church. The Deacon was passing out pizza to the children. I was feeling sick to my tummy and I told him I didn't want any pizza. Then he threw a slice of pizza onto the floor in front of all the other children and he told me to eat it. When I asked him "What?" He told me to get down on my knees and eat the slice of pizza.

I am sorry but I told him I am not a dog. I was so mad. I also cursed at him. I haven't been back to church since. He told me I couldn't come back until I wrote a letter of apology to him, but my teacher suggested I write it to you instead.

I hope God can forgive me and him too.
   Sincerely,
   Maria

Author Biography

Mark Wilkins
A Storyteller

My name is Mark Wilkins. I am best known to my readers as A Storyteller. I pen the A Storyteller Series of Books for Love Force International Publishing. Unlike most other book series, it does not concentrate on a particular character or a particular story line. Instead, it focuses on books of short stories in various genres by a particular author, namely myself. Some of the books in the A Storyteller Book Series include serious fiction (A Week's Worth of Fiction), humorous fiction (Slices of Life) and a mixture of serious and humorous fiction and non-fiction (Classroom Confessions) and supernatural Fiction (Stories of The Supernatural).

The readers who enjoy my books like reading that sparks their imagination. They like stories with memorable and quirky characters on unusual topics. They like unexpected twists and turns in the plot. If any of these things my readers enjoy describe you, then you too will enjoy my writing.

I am comfortable writing in many different genres. I write both humorous and serious fiction. Some of my stories are based on true events, others are totally my invention. It is up to you, the reader, to decide which stores are based on factual events and which are completely my invention because I'm not telling. I like to tell stories and I work very hard at making those stories both compelling and entertaining. I hope you enjoy reading my books.

Kindle Books by Loveforce International Publishing

Whether you are interested in true stories, fiction, humor, action, adventure, spiritual insights, quotes, poetry, self-help or children's books, Loveforce International Publishing has got you covered. **Our 99 cent commitment,** our commitment to a 99 cent (U.S.) price for all our kindle e book titles keep our books affordable. Since our books sell for the local equivalent of 99 cents (U.S.) in other global markets, people around the globe can afford them. Our books do sell all over the world. Our 99 cent commitment means there has never been a better time to stock up on books published by Love Force International! At a time when many paperbacks sell for $13.95-$17.95, our paperbacks sell for between $6.50-$7.50 (U.S.). This too is a bargain for our readers.

Many of the books listed here include their Amazon Kindle ASIN code. Typing an ASIN code into any Amazon search bar should bring that title up. If you are looking for titles published by Loveforce International Publishing you can simply type Loveforce International Publishing Company into any amazon search bar anywhere in the world and many of our books will come up. For books in Spanish type Loveforce Libros en Espanol into any Amazon search bar anywhere in the world.

Many of our books have Spanish Language versions. We didn't just slap the text onto Google Translate and pray. We worked with a professional Spanish translator born and raised in a Spanish speaking nation. We made our authors available to that person to clarify idioms and other translation glitches so that our Spanish versions are not only close to the original in meaning but they also fit within the culture(s) of Spanish Speaking nations.

We have some promotional videos for our books on Amazon Kindle. You can find many others on our You Tube channel The Loveforce International Publishing channel. Just type Loveforce International Publishing into your You Tube search bar anywhere in the world and the channel will come up along with many of our videos. Our logo is a photo of the sun coming out through a cloud over a mountain top. We have a Spanish Language You Tube Channel as well. Type Loveforce International Publishing en Espanol and you will see some of our Spanish language videos from our Loveforce enEspanol channel come up with the ones in English.

NOTE: Books with ASINs are available now the others will be available soon. All Titles are printed in English. Books with an **SP** after the title also have a version translated into Spanish. A List of Paperbacks will be below, Reader Series books with a paperback version will have **Ppr** on the same line as the title.

The Reader Series is a series of readers that are a sampling of writings by one or more authors.

The Prophet of Life Reader (7 Book Sampler) Volumes 1 & 2
What do essays, articles, stories, poetry and quotes have in common? They are all in this sampling of stories, poems and other writings from 7 of The Prophet of Life's writings found in these Kindle books.
Author: The Prophet of Life **ISBN: 978-1-936462-07-0**
ASIN: B015D716C0 (Vol 1) ASIN: B06XBSWKX8 (Vol 2)

The Mark Wilkins Reader 7 Book Sampler! Volumes 1 & 2
One story from seven books by Mark Wilkins. Whether its smart spouses, inquisitive fools, teachers, gangsters or ghosts these books give you a good sampling of stories by the man known throughout the world as A Storyteller. Within its pages you will find horror, humor and pathos.
Author: Mark Wilkins **ISBN: 978-1-936462-38-4**
ASIN: B01MU0Z51H Volume 1

The Love Force International Reader 7 Book Sampler! 4 Books in This Series

Whether you want fiction, humor, children's stories, poetry or quotes these books have got all of those and more! A sampling of 7 different books by three authors offered in Kindle books published by Love Force International.
Edited by Evan Lovefire   Vol 1 **ASIN:** B06XBHD9RX
Vol 2 **ASIN:** B06XBMGLNK
Vol 3 ASIN: B07DCGTLKF   Vol 4
ASIN: B07DP51BWG

The Love Force International Sampler, Spanish Books Edition SP Volumes 1 & 2
These books contain a sampling of 7 different books by three authors translated into Spanish. The books translated include What Faith has Taught me, Controversy, True Stories of Inspiration & General interest and Quotes about God by The Prophet of Life, Stories of The Supernatural, Slices of Life How to Become The Person You've Always Wanted by Mark Wilkins and Classic Children's Stories You've Likely Never Heard, and my first & second books of stupid little fables by Dr. Goose.
Edited by C. Gomez Vol 1 **ASIN:** B06XB3RJ2K Vol 2
ASIN:: B07F2PLVHF

The True Stories Series is a series of books which include true stories.

True Stories!   SP
A riveting collection of true stories. Whether you want to know about the toddler taken by a gator at a Disney Resort, an 18 year old who doesn't exist, which popular restaurant chain has a corporate mentality of public humiliation for its employees or an alarming new trend that could affect your household this book has got it all and they are all absolutely true!
Author: The Prophet of Life   **ISBN: 978-1-936462-16-2**
ASIN: B06XVSZSZ9

True Stories: Inspiration and General Interest
SP
What do cell phone addicts, George Orwell, birds, Paul McCartney, The Nobel Prize, Black Friday, Led Zeppelin, garbage, a pep talk, tipping, Steve Jobs, Shakespeare, inspirational thoughts and your mother have in common? They are in true stories in this book. True Stories of Inspiration & General Interest brings together stories and poems about celebrities, trends and everyday people. Sometimes surprising, always interesting, it will entertain you and give you something to think about at the same time.
Author: The Prophet of Life   **ISBN: 978-1-936462-15-5**
ASIN: B00TXWVNUC   ASIN: B01BBCKFZU
(Spanish Edition)

Controversy

Ppr SP

What do Caitlyn Jenner, Donald Trump, a cure for AIDS, Chinese hackers, Adolf Hitler and Global Warming have in common? They are all at the heart of a controversy and there are stories about them in this unique book that turns tabloid headlines inside out. **Author:** The Prophet of Life **ISBN: 978-1-936462-19-3 ASIN: B016MWU8NS ASIN: B01CRF3098 (Spanish Edition)**

True Stories of Crime and Punishment

SP

This book of serious crime stories is ripped from headlines all over the globe. From the family that vanished, to the 11 year old girl killed in a fight over a boy, to the prisoner who hasn't eaten in 14 years, to the severed human head found near the famous Hollywood sign these stories ripped will astound you and give you pause to think.
Author: The Prophet of Life **ISBN: 978-1-936462-17-9 ASIN: B01406YZBE ASIN: B01N10ND7S (Spanish Edition)**

Strange but True!

A collection of facts and stories about people, places and things that are strange and seem like fiction but are absolutely true!

Author: Mark Wilkins **ASIN:**

The A Storyteller Series is a unique book series. Instead of concentrating on a particular character or genre, the series consists of collections of short stories by Author Mark Wilkins, Also Known As A Storyteller.

The Slice of Life Series are books with humorous stories.

Slices of Life Volume 1
SP

is a collection of humorous short stories about life. Most of them deal with marriage and family members. From smart spouses to intelligent little children to guys trying to impress their friends and in-laws trying to master technology each story is like a little slice of life but together, they make up an irresistible pie. Sit back, grab a cup of coffee and enjoy some slices of lie because, before you know it, you will have finished the whole thing. **Author:** Mark Wilkins **ISBN: 978-1-936462-11-7 ASIN: B014ZF5VY0   ASIN: B01BBBZUL0 (Spanish Edition)**

Slices of Life Volume 2
SP

This sequel to Slices of Life has more humorous stories about the rich, the poor and the middle class. It even has a story about one of their pets. Ignorance is the main theme of this book, ignorance that has consequences that are sometimes touching but always humorous. So brew so coffee or tea, sit down and relax and enjoy another satisfying batch of more slice of life because, before you know it, you will have devoured the whole thing.

Author: Mark Wilkins **ISBN:** 978-1-936462-12-4 **ASIN:** B01M2B3YZ1 **ASIN:** B06XKP5C66 (Spanish Edition)

The Stories of The Supernatural Series are books with scary stories that cross the spectrum of Horror, Occult, Ghost, Monster and Fantasy genres.

Stories of The Supernatural Volume 1
SP
Ghosts, demonic creatures, and Death. This collection of Short Stories will haunt and entertain you. Whether it's the classic evil of A Lump of Coal or the whimsy of A Ghost in the House this collection of Short Stories and poems will haunt, thrill and entertain you.
Author: Mark Wilkins **ISBN:** 978-1-936462-18-6
ASIN: B01M1N1QR5 **ASIN:** B01MA12YXY
(Spanish Edition)

Stories of The Supernatural Volume 2
SP
In this sequel to Stories of The Supernatural there are more Ghosts, Demonic Creatures and Death. This collection of short stories Centers of Ghosts and Monsters. Within its pages you will marvel at the exploits of The Soul Collector, Shudder at the mention of the dreaded Bungadun and of the Hell Banger and ride the rails on the ghost train. Strap on your seat belts, it's going to be a bumpy ride! **Author:** Mark Wilkins **ISBN:** 978-1-936462-26-1
ASIN: B01MDJMSUY **ASIN:** B01M4FXDL1 **(Spanish Edition)**

A Storyteller Series Continued…
The A Week's Worth of Fiction Series is a series of books with seven stories of fiction each. Each book has stories organized by a particular theme. In a unique twist, each story is followed by a poem which has something indirectly to do with the story that came before it. Readers are asked to read one story and poem that follows it per day. This gives them one day to see how the story resonates with them and try and figure out how the poem is related to the story. To end the suspense, the author includes a section called "How the Poems in this Book are related to the Stories" at the end of the book.

A Week's Worth of Fiction Volume 1
SP

In Volume 1 of A Week's Worth of Fiction, People on The Edge, you will meet people on the edges of society. A security guard who struggles with a dying wife, an elderly man whose cast aside and left to die, one woman struggling to capture romance before her beauty fades and another struggling with cancer. You will meet a little boy who terrorizes a grocery store, a teenage boy searching for love and a small businessman struggling against a monopoly. If you want fictional stories you will never forget you only need to count to 7. **Author:** Mark Wilkins **ISBN: 978-1-936462-13-1**
ASIN: B01521SQ02   ASIN: B06XVD21PM (Spanish Edition)

A Week's Worth of Fiction Volume 2
SP

Volume 2 of A Week's Worth of Fiction, Science Fiction you will be intrigued and astounded by stories about a girl who has the cure for a deadly disease, a woman on a date with psycho somatic disease called prophecy, a robot chicken, a supernatural fly, an astral projection, a teacher in a new job where everything is not what it seems and a futuristic world where the only economy is barter. If you want science fiction stories you will never forget you only need to count to 7. **Author:** Mark Wilkins
ISBN: 978-1-936462-14-8 **ASIN:** **B01LX9RZH7**
ASIN: **B071GCYFK6** **(Spanish Edition)**

A Week's Worth of Fiction Volume 3
SP

A Week's Worth of Fiction Volume 3, The Many Sides of Violence, features 7 fictional stories that explore violence. One story looks at what goes through the mind of a terrorist about to blow himself up. Another, looks at an executive considering suicide. The plots of other stories include a, man trying to outwit an armed carjacker, a sky marshal trying to figure out which passage is a terrorist, a soldier who realizes someone in his platoon is a serial killer, an ex-convict who has to decide if he should use violence to combat evil and an everyman who becomes a hero through unspeakable violence, if you want violent stories you will never forget you only need to count to 7.**Author:** Mark Wilkins
ASIN: B071WNC6ZX   **ASIN:** **B072K6J9HN**
(Spanish Edition)

A Week's Worth of Fiction Volume 4
SP

In A Week's Worth of Fiction 4, Realizations, you will meet people from various backgrounds who come to important realizations. You will meet a Doctor who comes to a realization about old age, a politician who struggles to be his own man, a rich man who reaches an epiphany after a chance encounter at a store, A farmer in need of help, A little boy who struggles with a new cell phone that seems processed, a swimmer who gains insight from her morning routine and a police officer who develops empathy for a hardcore gangster. If you want the fictional stories you will never forget you only need to count to 7. **Author:** Mark Wilkins **ASIN: B07217QL6H   ASIN: B071JVQQ96   (Spanish Edition)**

A Storyteller series continued...

The Classroom Confessions Series is a series of books with stories from the front line of public education. Stories and song lyrics mostly focus on students and teachers. Some will make you laugh, others will make you cry but they will all give you insights into public education and entertain you while giving you something to think about.

Classroom Confessions Volume 1
        SP
is a series of true stories from the front lines of public education. Within its pages you will meet quirky characters, the good, the bad and the over caffeinated. Some of them are teachers, some students and some are administrators. Some will make you laugh, others will make you cry but they all play an important role in public education. Their stories are written in way that will entertain you and give you something to think about.
Author: Mark Wilkins **ISBN: 978-1-936462-08-7**
ASIN: B00VNFJBX8   ASIN: B01MSV4N92
(Spanish Edition)

Classroom Confessions Volume 2
                SP

Is another series of true stories from the front lines of public education. Within its pages you will meet unforgettable characters like the French Substitute, Mr. Happyhands, Harry Winkwater, The Bushwhacker and of course, Julian. Some will touch your heart, others will give you something to think about but they will all entertain you. **Author:** Mark Wilkins **ASIN: B01N1OCRVC ASIN: B06XC9HDQV (Spanish Edition)**

The Love Force Novella Series: These are short novels of varying length.

Karma Ppr SP

The story of one man who negotiates between two different cultures, and opposing life views competing for his attention. His conflicts and struggles are overshadowed by cosmic forces he cannot understand. Karma provides insights into the struggles and conflicts we all face. **Author: Mark Wilkins**

ASIN: B0722R448R (English Edition)
ASIN: B072Z6L36 (Spanish Edition)

The Beyond Faith Series

Is a series of books that look at life from a spiritual perspective. No matter what your faith, you will find spiritual insights in these books that will enrich your life.

What Faith Has Taught Me
SP
 I am just an ordinary person who has been privileged to have a life filled with miracles and revelations. There are many times when I had nothing except faith but faith was all I needed to sustain me. My faith and my God have taught me many life lessons. This book shares some of the things my faith has taught me and the spiritual insights I have gained because of my faith. **Author:** The Prophet of Life **ISBN: 978-1-936462-03-2 ASIN: B01527IKT8 ASIN: B01EE3QSW2   (Spanish Edition)**

Finding God in A Chaotic World   SP
The world can seem so chaotic these days. Many people long for guidance. Many others want to get closer to God. How do you find God amidst the chaos and confusion? How can you discern God's messages from the multi-media blitz we are each bombarded with every day? Some people are part of an organized religion. Others are spiritual without a particular religion. Some are still searching, All of them trying to find God.

In this book, you will learn that The Lord communicates with how The Lord communicates with you. You will learn about the True Nature of God and realize just how profound God's Love and reach are. You will learn the secret of why God's will always prevails. If you are ready for revelations that may change the way you look at life in general and your life in particular, read this book.
Author: The Prophet of Life **ISBN: 978-1-936462-01-8**
ASIN: B00SLLZAAU
ASIN: B0793KDYX3 (Spanish Edition)

Finding God without Religion   **SP**
People of faith are not exclusive to religion. There are many who are spiritual or agnostic. They don't fit into the doctrine, rituals and congregational community of religion. In this wisdom filled volume, people of faith but without an organized religion can gain insights into life, the afterlife and God without being brow beaten or guilt tripped into conversion. This volume is Book 2 of the Revelations of 2012 Beyond Faith series. Part 1 is entitled Finding God in A Chaotic World.
Author: The Prophet of Life **ISBN: 978-1-936462-10-0**
ASIN: B00XKPD86K   **ASIN: B07F5MTFVQ (Spanish Edition)**

Inspiration For All 1
        SP

Selected Inspirational Writings. Whether you are of faith or just in need of inspiration in your life, this book full of inspirational stories, poems and essays will sustain and strengthen you on your journey. **Authors: The Prophet of Life & Mark Wilkins ASIN: B071ZM17V6 ASIN: B071JW8XXH (Spanish Edition)**

Inspiration for All 2
       SP
This is a book of selected inspirational writings by three different authors. It will not only entertain you but will also stimulate your mind by offering you alternative ways of looking at things and opportunities to gain insights. **Authors**: Mark Wilkins, The Prophet of Life & Dr. Goose. **ASIN: B0736JH6M9**   **ASIN: B072WK9JBH (Spanish Edition)**

Outrageous Humor Series
Books of stories and fake news articles for those with an off-beat sense of humor.

Outrageous Stories   SP
This book is filled with offbeat humor articles. All of them are fictitious and many of them completely outrageous. No one is safe from being made fun of be they terrorists, Presidents, Dictators, The Movie and Record Business or couch potatoes. If you are college age or older and have an offbeat, irreverent, sense of humor, this book is for you!
Author: Mark Wilkins **ISBN: 978-1-936462-33-9**
ASIN: B01LY3VZJR
ASIN: B07D1RH9W3 (Spanish Edition)

More Outrageous Stories   SP
This book is filled with more offbeat humor articles. All of them are fictitious and many of them completely outrageous. No one is safe from being made fun of be they terrorists, Racists, National Holidays or the medical establishment. If you are college age or older and have an offbeat, irreverent, sense of humor, this book is for you!
Author: Mark Wilkins **ISBN: 978-1-936462-33-9**
ASIN: B074Y8LTTJ

Self Help Series
This consists of books by different authors designed to help people improve their lives.

Become The Person You've Always Wanted to Be
SP

This self-help book offers a simple, yet profound method of making positive changes in your life. It includes a link to download exclusive, helpful companion worksheets to help you become the person you have always wanted to be. **Author:** Mark Wilkins **ISBN:** 978-1-936462-39-1 ASIN: B01MSYVAB6   ASIN: B01MSYVU6R   (Spanish Edition)

Life Success Kit   SP
Spiritual Thought Leader The Prophet of Life helps you clarify what success really means to you through a series of inspirational life lessons designed to give you new perspectives on achieving success and a blueprint for making changes in the things that are preventing you from becoming a success.
Author: The Prophet of Life **ASIN:** B01MZ2TSCP
    ASIN: B078JZGWDH (Spanish Edition)

The Your Life in Rhyme Poetry Series

Is a series of Poetry books unlike any you have ever read whether it is an exploration of life itself through a thematic chapter on each of the various stages of life as in Reflections in The Mirror of Life, The mixture of thought provoking essays and inspirational poetry of Black in America or the exploration of a single topic as in Romance Returns or Life in Verse. The books in this series will have you rediscovering poetry in a way that will make you wonder why you ever avoided it in the first place.

Reflections in the Mirror of Life

This unique book explores life through its harsh realities, pleasant diversions and positive possibilities. The book looks at modern society, the problems it faces, and the people who are a part of it. In a unique twist that's different from most books of poetry, Reflections is divided into five chapters, each of which explores a different theme woven into the fabric of modern life. The tone for each chapter is set by a free verse poem which is followed by a series of rhyming poems on that theme.

Author: The Prophet of Life **ISBN: 978-1-936462-04-9 ASIN: B00V2TSAXC**

Black in America

is an exploration of racism through essays and poems. It spans from the beginnings of the Civil Rights movement through today. It looks at people who have been lightning rods for race relations in America and has some surprising insights into the people and events that have shaped race relations in America for the past 60 years. This book is a good companion for anyone who wants to gain insight into the Civil Rights movement, race relations and racism itself.   **Author:** The Prophet of Life
ISBN: 978-1-936462-09-4   ASIN: B00S05QSXA

Every Lyric Tells A Story   SP
- A collection of unique song lyrics that tell compelling stories about people, their lives, their hopes and dreams. You can find yourself and people you know in many of them. **Authors:** The Prophet of Life & Mark Wilkins   **ASIN: B01NAFDWZW**
ASIN: B07F5N1Y5G (Spanish Edition)

Romance Lives!
Romance Lives is a very special collection of Romantic Love Poems. The poems are arranged to follow the arc of a romance from its early, puppy love stages through its sweet seductions and the blissful wisdom of mature love. If you are searching for Romance in your love relationship or just want some joyful, insightful romantic reading this book is for you! **Authors: The Prophet of Life & Mark Wilkins ASIN: B07D9WY6V5**
ASIN: B07DP7HX9P (Spanish Edition)

Life in Verse

A collection of poems about life. The poems and song lyrics are about people, their lives, their hopes and dreams. You can find yourself and people you know in many of them. **Author:** The Prophet of Life **ASIN:**

The Best Quotes quotation series
Is a series of books filled with quotes attributed to the
Prophet of Life whose quotes have been used by charities,
corporations, institutions of Medicine and higher learning.
The book includes a license to use any of the quotes as
long as they are attributed to The Prophet of Life.

The Best Quotes About God   **SP**
This short book is filled with some of the more popular
quotes about God attributed to The Prophet of Life. It is
both thought provoking and inspirational. It is filled with
dozens of quotes about God that one can read and copy for
personal use.   **Author:** The Prophet of Life **ISBN: 978-
1-936462-20-9 ASIN: B018P0M8OC   ASIN:
B01BJXYHLY (Spanish Edition)**

The Best Quotes on General Subjects
    SP
This short book is filled with some of the more popular
quotes on general subjects attributed to The Prophet of
Life. The book includes quotes on topics such as life, love,
happiness, crime and punishment, wellness and includes
many of the humorous quotes attributed to The Prophet of
Life. You will find the wit and wisdom in its pages thought
provoking and inspirational. It is filled with dozens of
quotes about God that one can read and copy for personal
use.

Author: The Prophet of Life   ASIN: B01M58L9LW
ASIN: B01M58L9LW (Spanish Edition)

The Best Spiritual Quotes
SP

This book is filled with some of the more popular quotes on Spiritual Subjects attributed to The Prophet of Life. Included are quotes on faith, mercy, life lessons, humanity and spirituality. You should find them to be profound, thought provoking and inspirational. It is filled with many pages of quotes that one can read and copy for personal use. **Author:** The Prophet of Life
ASIN: B01MQVA87Q   **ASIN: B07DP68YSF**
(Spanish Edition)

Children's Storybook Series
All books are by Dr. Goose who writes in both prose and rhyming verse.

Classic Children's Stories You've Likely Never Heard SP
Help develop your child's creative abilities and develop their imagination by reading them stories from this book that has no illustrations. Whether it's a story about Prince trying to find the answer to a question, a spider talking about a savior, a kingdom in trouble or a child trying to save the world you will find yourself wanting to read these children's stories with international flavor again and again. This first book in the series is for smaller children.
Author: Dr. Goose **ISBN:** 978-1-936462-40-7
ASIN: B01NAF8QNU   **ASIN:** B01MR5PR84   **(Spanish Edition)**

More Classic Children's Stories You've Likely Never Heard   SP
This sequel gives you more unknown classics. The book introduces new characters like a little chicken whose life is similar to a person's and a ballad about a hairy man. There is a story about a prince whose refusal causes an international incident. There is even an updated version of classic children's story everyone knows from different character's points of view. This second book in the series helps tweens and juvenile children creative abilities and develop their imagination as stories from this book that has no illustrations either. **Author:** Dr. Goose **ISBN:** 978-1-936462-41-4

ASIN: B074Y8G4JZ   ASIN:
B0755YK6NH   (Spanish Edition)

My First Book of Stupid Little Fables   SP
Whether the greed of mooches and lunch thieves, sadistic
children, or bizarre stories about pets this first installment
in the series of irreverently humorous stories with twisted
endings about the selfish and the greedy delivers. It even
has the stupid little drawings! For Juveniles. **Author:** Dr.
Goose
ISBN: 978-1-936462-44-5   ASIN: B07FFCNCQZ
ASIN: B07FFF13N4 (Spanish Edition)

My Second Book of Stupid Little Fables   SP
Whether it's well-meaning but incompetent grandmas,
egotistical women, sadistic children, or crazy people in
shopping centers, this second installment in the series of
irreverently humorous stories with twisted endings about
the selfish and the greedy delivers. It even has the
drawings you love to make fun of just like the first one!
For Juveniles. **Author:** Dr. Goose   **ISBN:**
ASIN: **ASIN:**   **(Spanish**
Edition)

More Children's Stories
School Kidz Volume 1 Elementary and Middle School
SP
Six funny stories about kids who are smarter than their
age. Within its pages you will meet A boy whose
vocabulary is better than the adults in his school, a kid who
escapes a spanking, A kid who gets a new cell phone with
a built in problem and a brother and sister who learn how
get rid of junk from an old aunt. Recommended for kidz
ages 12-16. **Author:** Mark Wilkins **ASIN: B0717B6SQ4**

ASIN: B078JMR7ZB (Spanish Edition)

School Kidz Volume 2 High School   **SP**
9 stories about kids who are in high school. Within its pages you will meet a group of Kidz who get involved in a rotten egg war, a girl who doesn't exist, and a kid who sends a friend on a date with his sister. Recommended for kidz ages 14-18. **Author:** Mark Wilkins **ASIN: B071W5WZZN**

Coming Soon E Workbooks and an E Textbook!
A series of mini and one comprehensive E Textbook Under the title of Mr. Wilkins Teaches English by Mark Wilkins

The specific mini textbooks will be on topics such as Reading and Responding to Literature, and Methods for Writing Paragraphs and Essays. The Comprehensive text will include a weekly spelling component and both the mini texts and comprehensive Text will include creative lessons that promote creativity and critical thinking in students while fitting into common core standards. The mini texts will be no more than 99 cents each and the comprehensive text will be paperback for under $10!
 All of the books are freshly created and contain exclusive intellectual property you won't find in any other texts. These books are perfect for students learning high school English levels 9 & 10 whether you are a classroom teacher or are home schooling your child. We are making the commitment to keep all of the books at low prices to allow parents and school districts to afford texts in the face of shrinking educational budgets. Purchasers will be given an opportunity to receive an email with a printable version of the exercises and assignments as well as links to online testing free of charge.
Author: Mark Wilkins   **ISBN:**   **ASIN:**

Compelling Stories for Adaptation to Short Film
For Film Students

Compelling stories in a set location with six or less characters. Easily adaptable to screenplay with notes on adapting them.
Author: Mark Wilkins   **ISBN:**   **ASIN:**

Loveforce Paperbacks

All of our paperback books cost between $6.50 and $7.50.

Stories of The Supernatural: A Storyteller Series

Book SP Loveforce Duo

This collection of 15 stories is filled with ghosts, demonic creatures, monsters and death. It will haunt you, thrill you and entertain you. Within its pages you will marvel at the exploits of The Soul Collector and the uniqueness of Life Lines and Cannibal Money. You will shudder at the mention of a lump of coal or the dreaded Bungadun of Blood Valley and ride the rails on the ghost train. Strap on your seat belts, it's going to be a bumpy ride! **Author:** Mark Wilkins

ISBN-13: 978-1936462537   ISBN-13: 978-1936462575 SP

Karma   SP

Karma is the story of one man who negotiates between two different cultures, and opposing life views competing for his attention. His conflicts and struggles are overshadowed by cosmic forces he cannot understand. Karma provides insights into the struggles and conflicts we all face.

Author: Mark Wilkins   **ISBN-13: 978-1936462506**
ISBN-13: 978-1936462582 SP

A Week's Worth of Fiction Volumes 1 & 2
SP   Loveforce Duo

Whether it's people on the edges of society or Science Fiction Stories, this collection of Volumes 1 & 2 of A Week's Worth of Fiction gives you 2 volumes each with 7 stories that will thrill you, surprise you and make you think. Often dystopic and sometimes surreal, if you want stories you will never forget you only need to count to 7 and you can do it twice in this special paperback edition.

Author: Mark Wilkins **ISBN-13: 978-1936462551**

Totally Outrageous Stories! Outrageous Satire
Loveforce Trio

There is absolutely nothing that escapes ridicule in this flagrantly outrageous, biting satire of everything you can imagine. This smart, flippant book pokes fun at the entertainment industry, the medical establishment, politics, societal norms, history and science. If you want to laugh to humor with no mercy, you have to get totally outrageous!
Author: Mark Wilkins   **ISBN-10:** 1936462494   **ISBN-13:** 978-1936462490

Slices of Life: Stories of Humor and Pathos (A Storyteller Series)   SP Loveforce Duo

Slices of Life Slices is a collection of humorous short stories about life. Most of them deal with marriage and family members. There are smart spouses, intelligent little children, guys trying to impress their friends and in-laws trying to master technology. Ignorance is the main theme of this book, ignorance that has consequences that are sometimes touching but always humorous. Each story is like a little slice of life but together, they make up an irresistible pie. Sit back, grab a cup of coffee and enjoy some slices of life because, before you know it, you will have finished the whole thing.
Author: Mark Wilkins   **ISBN-13: 978-1936462452 ISBN-13: 978-1936462469 SP**

Public School Confessions: Stories From The Front Lines of Public Education Loveforce Duo SP

Teachers, students and administrators come to life and often clash in dozens of stories from the front lines of public education. Within these pages you will meet people who are smart, rebellious and over caffeinated. Some stories will make you laugh, some will make you cry but they will also entertain you and make you think. **Author:** Mark Wilkins **ISBN-13: 978-1936462056   ISBN-13: 978-1936462063 SP**

The Faith Trilogy   SP   Loveforce Trio

• This Faith Trilogy Paperback includes three faith filled books: What Faith Has Taught Me, The Best Quotes About God and Inspiration for All: Selected Inspirational Writings. **Author:** Mark Wilkins **ISBN-13: 978-1936462513   ISBN-13: 978-1936462520 (Spanish Edition)**

The Agnostic Faith Trilogy   SP   Loveforce Trio
Three great books combined in one paperback book! You get: Finding God without Religion, The Best Spiritual Quotes and Finding god in a Chaotic World. **Author:** The Prophet of Life
ISBN-13: 978-1936462476   ISBN-13: 978-1936462599 (Spanish Edition)

Black in America
Black in America is an exploration of racism in America through essays and poems. It spans from the beginnings of the civil rights movement through today, It includes powerful new poems "Why We Say Black Lives Matter", "Baltimore", "Requiem for Laquan" It takes a look at people who have been lightning rods for race relations in America and has some surprising insights into the people and events that have shaped race relations in America for the past 60 years. It is a powerful work that teaches as it entertains and allows the reader gain new insights.
Author: The Prophet of Life
ISBN-13: 978-1936462025

Controversies
     SP

What do Caitlyn Jenner, Donald Trump, Hollywood
Sex Scandals, a cure for AIDS, Chinese hackers,
Adolf Hitler and Global Warming have in common?
They are all at the heart of a controversy and there
are stories about them in this unique book that turns
tabloid headlines inside out.

Author: Mark Wilkins **ISBN-13: 978-1936462483**